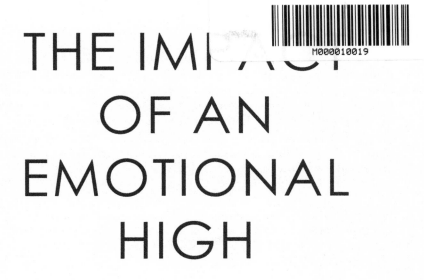

THE IMPACT OF AN EMOTIONAL HIGH

How to Talk about Bipolar Disorder with Your Family

Jen Kraakevik

Positively Powered Publications

Positively Powered Publications
PO Box 270098
Louisville, CO 80027
PositivelyPoweredPublications.com

Cover Design: Melody Christian of FinickyDesigns.com
Proofreading Editor: Jennifer Bisbing
Photos: Jessica Baskett Photography

Quantity sales: Special discounts are available on quantity purchases by nonprofit organizations, corporations, associations, clubs and others. For details, contact us at PositivelyPoweredPublications.com

The Impact of an Emotional High/Jennifer Kraakevik —1st ed.
ISBN: 978-1-954479-99-9

Dedication

To my loving family: thanks for being people who make dreams come true.

To my dad: I love you always, with or without bipolar disorder. You make me so proud.

Foreword

By John Kraakevik

IN JANUARY 2017, MY DAUGHTER JEN emailed me about another one of her writing projects, and I was expecting to help her edit it. Instead, she had an idea for a book about mental illness. She had taken a special interest and wanted to write about it.

The problem was, she wanted to write about mine.

At first, I wondered what my personal experience could add to a plethora of coming-outs. All that could be said probably has been said, and quite eloquently. I was not a talk show host or movie star, filmmaker or artist. I was just an ordinary guy floating in and out of employment. My wife had supported the family for years. I had applied twice for disability, finally being approved for it in 1990. By that time, I had decided, for me, disability wasn't financially feasible and a terrible strategy. I wanted to get better, not just survive.

That was the year I went up to Mayo Clinic on my second wild ride through mania. That was two years after Jen was born. For decades, I could not tell my kids the real story. I was the "stay at home dad" long before general acceptance. The kids wore hand-me-downs from their cousins. My sister-in-law and her husband co-signed on our mortgage. My brother-in-law said, "I didn't know people could even live on this." Although finances were tight, that was the least of our problems.

Socially, we felt isolated. Emotionally, we were exhausted. I couldn't bear to bring this to another generation. I felt almost everything was dependent on people not knowing I was bipolar. If the kids even whispered "mental illness," the few neighborhood kids would never come over. I would never be able to find a full-time job because "the word" would be out. It was a horrible secret, a shaming, and as a later job counselor would say, "Something you can't fix." His wife was bipolar. Not exactly encouraging words.

I knew a few people who were bipolar—a young mother whose husband refused to believe in her illness, and a very successful businessman who collapsed one day and has been on disability ever since, and a dozen others who attended the local mental illness chapter.

But I had never met, never seen, or expected to see anyone who was bipolar hold a full-time job and contribute. That was not my social strata. I had read somewhere that you would only have success if you attained it before you were diagnosed. These are all ignorant ideas.

But this is really Jen's story. When I was in and out of hospitals, when I lost jobs and stayed at home, when I went around the house crying for no reason or laid around sleeping, my daughter was there. I went through the disease, but she lived it.

She is not my psychiatrist. Not my spouse. Not my boss.

Just a daughter who has the courage to ask questions and force me to examine my own experiences. And that's how it all began, with letters to my daughter.

Table of Contents

Introduction

The Impact of an Emotional High gives light to what happens in a family when someone is diagnosed with bipolar disorder. The discovery. The hurt. The frustration. Over and over and over again. The impact isn't solely trauma that happened in the past, the impact continues as our family member continues to live through it. It's not over, but it can be dealt with. So, how do we deal with it? How do we allow something that is unconscious in our families (like the nature of bipolar disorder) to not have the same impact over and over on us? I know it's not over for you, or you wouldn't be reading this book.

We who are affected by it don't have a choice. We have a family member who has it. It changes us and the way we look at the world.

So, what is there to do about it? What if you had options?

Having someone in your family living with bipolar disorder is a part of you, and you can achieve greatness in spite of it, and even because of it. You do not have to use it as an excuse for not reaching your goals, but rather, you can find your superpower within it and through it.

My name is Jen Kraakevik. By no means am I a psychologist, nor a mental health expert. This book is not intended to substitute for medical advice, and you should always consult with a physician in matters relating to your health and the health of your family members, especially as it relates to any symptoms requiring diagnosis or medical attention.

In fact, I wanted to be the "average Joe" as the author of this book. I didn't want a psychology or doctor title because I believe that we, as average people, need each other to know what to do, how to relate, and decide where to go next. Together. Through this book, I reveal the circumstances and my own emotions of dealing with my dad's mental illness, in hopes that we can all be free of its devastating effects on us and our families.

In spite of my "no-expert" status, I do have experience. Thirty years of living and being surrounded by bipolar disorder. The natural ups and downs of life are exacerbated by this mental illness. My experience occurred with the father I turn to in times of struggle, the one who supports and loves me.

With that, I definitely don't know everything by writing this book. I believe it's one of the pitfalls we can fall into with reading books. By believing that authors know everything about their topics, we can forget their humanity and also put them in a category of "better than me," simply because they have authority or published a book. Doing that could take away from the connection and the power that you have with your life. By reading this book, I never want to pretend like I know it all because I don't know your life, I only know what has worked well for me. I know I haven't "conquered" understanding bipolar disorder, haven't "figured out" how it goes, nor do I know how to talk about it completely. I don't expect myself to either. I took time to explore it. That's all. And, I share this story because I want you to be able to do the same within your community, if you so choose.

Another pitfall I worry about is thinking that this is all over if you read this book or communicate a few times "effectively" with family members. I'm never sure I'm doing it "right," and question if I have a full awareness of my own mental state or whether I'll recognize what is going on with my dad. It's not really over, even if I wish it was. We can only try our best. Same goes with our family members.

I hope you make the time to explore and debunk this myth through my lens.

In my childhood (and continuing into adulthood), I noticed the inconsistencies that came with Dad disappearing for periods of time, or spending hours staring out the window. Sometimes Dad would sleep for over twelve hours a day or go buy a car without consulting my mom. Other times, my parents would fight hard about money because Dad had done something that no one could have anticipated. I also clearly remember the day I could finally separate bipolar disorder as the mental health diagnosis and not my dad.

I'm lucky because my family member, my dad, is still in my life. I'm sure that is not the case for some of you. Unlike mine, your parents may not still be together. You may not be in touch with your brother, sister, mother, father, cousin, aunt, grandparent, your family member or friend who is diagnosed with a mental illness. Perhaps your family member passed away, and you are looking to grieve. Maybe you have the diagnosis, and you want to know your family member's perspective. You may not have the words you feel you need. I didn't have them either. Your experience is unique to you and your family, and is not to be discredited.

Through your experience, I want you to know that you're not alone, even if it feels like you have been or if you literally have been. Especially if you can't imagine talking with anyone about what you have been through. I was there. I didn't talk about it either. Don't worry, that's normal. You're normal.

My family could never live up to my expectations of the "perfect" family I had envisioned. As I grow up, I see more how that was a fabrication and that this vision of family was, in fact, impossible. Every day, I experience how amazing, loving, caring, and forgiving my family actually is. I am extremely grateful for their willingness to deal with and respond to whatever I have wanted to talk about. In the last couple of years, it has been the context of this book and bipolar disorder. I decided we would talk through structured, recorded conversations (interviews) and through a writing project with my dad. Graciously, they agreed and helped me understand more about this illness and about themselves. Dad and I wrote countless pages of our journeys while I asked questions I'd never dreamed he'd actually answer. These are the letters to my daughter he referred to in the foreword. What I gleaned from sharing with him and interviewing my immediate family and my uncles (Dad's brothers) is what you have in front of you. These pages are the story, the teaching moments, and the resources I've discovered in this process of writing a book.

I intentionally brought "all of the feels" in the first section, my story, so that you can feel your way through those emotions with me. I include questioning which emotion I was feeling, and the way my emotions consistently showed up as tears. I hope you can access your own emotions through my examples.

In the second section, I outline exactly what I did to start a conversation with my family. We didn't talk about mental health much when I was a kid, so this is what I did to bring it up as an adult. It may be what you need if you are in that stage, ready to talk.

The last part is the resources I have compiled about bipolar disorder and other mental illnesses. I believe these resources can support you as you continue loving your family member and yourself.

This illness has had its effect on us. Bipolar disorder can be very hard to understand, and the specific symptoms vary from person to person. That is why I believe our stories should be out there. We need to share, and we need each other to have all aspects of the illness expressed. Perhaps we can't express them all ourselves, but as a community, we may begin to grasp the complexity of bipolar disorder. That can't happen without sharing, so there will be an invitation to join a community at the end of this book. This is where

Dad and I invite you and your family members to connect with us and our communities in a simple way.

Use this book as you need to. Please take your time.

Before we jump in, I have to warn you about a few things.

- My story includes many Christian references. Bear with them if you are not of that religious tradition—I'm not either anymore. Jesus Christ and praying were important parts of how I processed what was going on in my life at the time. Try to not to let it take away from your own experience or how you can relate to my story.

- You will see I used the word "crazy" when I first discover my dad's illness. I used this word to help me make sense of it. I do not think my dad is crazy, nor do I promote the word "crazy" to use for anyone diagnosed with bipolar disorder or other mental illness. I decided not to cut it out because it shows my process and a process (I think) that is common among us. As you read these parts, please be gracious with me for that early conversation as I worked out over time how not crazy my dad is.

- Lastly, I changed some names and identifying details to preserve the privacy of my family and my community. This story is true and is my perspective of how bipolar disorder showed up in my life and does not reflect the views of anyone else in my family except me.

I want healing for my family, and in succession, for your family. By family, I mean your genetically predisposed/married-in family or your chosen family of friends and community members. I will refer to "family" throughout the book as either version because I believe that families can encompass more than genetics. My family is important to me, and I know you're reading this book because yours is too.

While writing this, I was committed to picking apart trauma. This trauma wasn't intentional. It just was what it was. I want you to have access to seeing what trauma you have in your past, especially regarding your family member's bipolar disorder. As a result, I hope you can see the possibility of freedom. I aspire that this book brings freedom from upset about this continuing disease and gives you access to a new future.

My goal is to encourage people with family members diagnosed with bipolar disorder to express their concerns within the family. I hope to meet you where you are so that you can access your voice in a way you never have before. With our stories out in the world, I want no one to die from a mental illness ever again.

And by saying that, I would love for us also to approach mental illness with the mentality of "nothing's wrong." I try my best to point out my uncertainty throughout the book as I thought that something was wrong with me or my dad with this illness. In the discovery, you'll see how that changes and that I begin to see that all of this is a part of life.

I truly hope this is the help you've been looking for. Let's start this journey together to transform and set ourselves free from any limitations we have surrounding bipolar disorder.

Thanks for joining me. And welcome to my family.

SECTION I: MY STORY

CHAPTER ONE

The First Episode
(That I Saw)

"WHAT DID YOU SAY, DAD?"

"I'm not going to be around much longer. I love you."

I couldn't help the tears that fell down my face. I hid them behind my obnoxious yellow sweatshirt as we stood by the front door. *What does he mean? Why is he saying that?*

I was only seventeen. He'd been there for everything in my life. He loved and cared about me. As far as I knew, he was invincible. A little quirky perhaps, but invincible. Definitely not going to die. *Was he telling me something he knew? Are my parents breaking up? Why does he have that weird gaze in his eyes, like he knows everything?*

"Where are you going?" The words came out of my brother Dan's mouth now. He spoke of our uncertainty. He spoke what I couldn't. Those darn tears.

"Don't you think God wants you to be here with your family?" Mom chimed in as she heard our questioning. She must have heard Dad's declaration from the kitchen. We then heard the "clunk" of the stockpot Mom set on the dining room table. The clinking of the soup spoons on bowls resounded, Mom setting the table, as Dad waited to respond. The drop of the water hit the glasses Mom was now filling, going back-and-forth from the kitchen to the dining room. *Why wasn't she taking this seriously?*

"It's not important. I love you, and I'm going away."

Two glasses in hand, Mom hushed him, moving quickly through the open layout of our house, circling past the front foyer where we were, and said, "You don't have to go anywhere right now. Just sit down for dinner."

She motioned to the dining room area. He smiled mischievously as we all walked together to the table. He sat right where she gestured. *Is he a kid pouting his way into submission? Forced by Mom's glare? We all know of Mom's "look," but when has Dad ever reacted like this?*

Pretty soon, my brother was going for seconds on the soup, and I was too. We both ate a lot. Looking at Dad before shoveling the next bite of food into my mouth, I noticed he was quiet and hadn't touched anything.

"Dad, are you going to eat?" I asked.

He immediately blurted, "I'm going on a mission from God."

"What?" I looked at my brother for confirmation. *Was that weird? Is he doing it again?* My heartbeat went faster and faster, my eyebrows furrowed in confusion. Being sixteen months apart had made us pretty close. We could sometimes read each other, especially in a state like this, with confusion and weirdness. He knew I was going to cry, and I knew that he would be logical. It had always been that way. My eyes immediately watered up, again.

"Earthly things like eating aren't important anymore. I have to follow God." He got up to leave. I grabbed his hand.

"It's okay, Dad, you can just sit here." He kept moving. "Dad," I pleaded, tears on my cheeks now, "Just sit."

None of it made any sense. We always ate together for family dinners, lunches, and breakfasts on the weekends when possible. Dad would *always* eat. What was different about today? All of a sudden, he had a "mission from God"? We all believed in God. God sent his Son to die on the cross for our sins. But, this "mission" specifically, unless it was to spread the gospel of Jesus Christ, no one else knew. *What is happening?*

"Well, why don't you just eat first? Then, you can focus on this 'mission.'" Mom gave her opinion nonchalantly, sarcasm dripping ever so slightly. She didn't bat an eye. Same as before. She didn't give in to him like I was by freaking out (and tearing up). Maybe she hoped that her flippancy would help Dad ignore his mission. Maybe it could convince him of how irrational this was. Maybe she was annoyed because this wasn't her first experience with this. Maybe she didn't know what to do with us watching every move they both made.

The questions started pouring out of Dad's mouth.

"Why should I eat this? What if God doesn't want me to eat this soup? What if it's actually the devil convincing me to eat this?"

An abstract smile emerged as he waited smugly for our responses. Each answered in its appropriate time. Emotion built up within me. Confusion. Distrust. Uncertainty. *Why question God this way? Did Dad call us devilish because we told him to eat?*

Jaw dropped, mouth ajar, eyes welling up with tears, I tried to stop them from sliding down my cheeks. I couldn't hide it. I never really could. I turned my head and wiped my eyes. This wasn't Dad. He would never try to trick someone. He wouldn't be questioning God like this. My dad was solid in his faith. I was the young person struggling to face the questions of life at seventeen. This sounded more like me.

I'd been questioning what I believed about Jesus since I was thirteen when I was challenged by someone I thought was my friend. I'd been trying to overcome doubt because I believed it was wrong to even talk about it. I knew I had to push through it to continue to believe in God. Dad was the opposite. In my eyes, he had the answers. He'd believed for years, his whole life and my whole life. I strove to have all of the answers like he did, especially in my faith. *Where is this Dad now?*

Dad was a devout Christian who cared significantly about his life and his relationship with his Savior. He cared about family, showed up to basketball games, choir concerts, and piano recitals. He cheered on the sidelines as he watched me run in circles on a black rubber track. I would wake up in the morning and catch him reading the Bible, drinking his coffee most days. We prayed before every meal, thanking Him for our food. Prayer, God, and family were important in our lives.

Besides that, I heard stories of him writing letters to Mom when they dated long distance. We frequently met up with family, and he was always there. He took us to the park and cooked us Swedish pancakes on Saturday mornings. He was studious and responsible. He had lists of things to do, and he did them. He didn't worry himself about the petty stuff like whether to eat. So who was this man? I didn't understand why there was a fight to keep him at the dinner table. A fight to keep him focused. A fight to get him to eat. *What is going on?*

We hadn't talked a lot about the devil's work because we focused on God and his provisions for our family. Mom would tell us stories of when we didn't have any money, especially when we were younger. She would remind us of the times He provided for us with clothes, cars, etc. I had even gone to go to church camp almost every summer, which for our family was a miracle, especially with how I thought our finances looked. So none of what was happening with Dad made any sense.

He stood up again. What was the point of staying at the table if he had a mission? He had to get ready for his "purpose." *But where are we in this purpose? Would he abandon us? Is he going to kill himself on this "mission"? Why doesn't he tell us more?*

One of my best friend's sisters had tried to kill herself. When my friend told me about it, it barely registered. I never understood why someone would think that suicide was the solution. *Was Dad someone I couldn't understand now? Could God direct my dad to commit suicide? That doesn't sound like the God I knew.* I never thought my friend's stories would play out right in my living room. I never would have considered that one of my family members could potentially end his life or disappear forever.

"John Mark," Mom said sternly. She knew he was scaring us, especially me. Maybe he was scaring her too. She had to say something. He heard her voice and sat back down. My voice emerged in explanation. Finally.

"Well, Dad, God would want you to receive nourishment from the soup that we're having. He wants you and all of us to be healthy and strong."

I had done a good job. Concise. And I explained the health advantages that we derived from food. *Great job, Jen!* I always prided myself on doing good work and getting As in school.

Dad looked up at me, spoon in hand, a dabble of soup on it because my brother had forced him to put his spoon into his bowl. I couldn't use being smart in this circumstance. He ignored it. That explanation wasn't good enough. *I'm not good enough.* Immediately, unconsciously, I turned away.

I could see something in his eyes I didn't want to see: the certainty that he was right. No one could explain correctly. No one could beat him. He was invincible. This invincibility was something I had never seen from Dad before. It was outside of himself, bigger than him, and came from some place I'd never seen before. *Is this the devil in Dad?*

He sat there, not eating his soup. Like a child refusing to eat his vegetables. Like a teenager rebelling against what his parents asked. Asking "why" to the extent that perhaps he'd resorted to his three-year-old self in adult form. I became quiet. I couldn't say anything. Nothing would make a difference. I was helpless.

"Fine, Dad, how about you just have some water? You don't have to eat… drink some water, and you'll feel better." My brother hoped to reassure him he was okay. Maybe he was thirsty, perhaps dehydrated from this afternoon? We could all survive on just water, and Dad could skip a meal, no problem. *Is this where we should focus our attention?*

Dad stared at us as he lifted the glass to his lips. He pretended to take a sip, and then he set it right back down, with the water at the exact same level. *Really, Dad?*

"This isn't important. I don't need this," He repeated.

Over and over, we watched him "fake us out." He was playing a game. *Why is he messing with us?*

Then he moved out of his chair again.

"Wait, Dad, come on," I spoke again, urging Dad to stay. I moved over to the chair closest to him and pulled his arm back towards his seat, hand clutched in desperation.

This wasn't okay. *What is wrong with him?* I looked at Mom as my brother continued to reason with him. I couldn't anymore. Something was desperately wrong. I was stunned that this conversation didn't have anything to do with anything we normally talked about. I was filled with uncertainty. My dad's face caused my emotion, or so I thought.

My brother didn't give up so quickly. Patiently, he gave Dad all of the reasons water was important: it's essential to live; our bodies are made up of 90% water, etc.

Dad was intelligent; he read books in his spare time, all sorts of books on history and science. He wasn't the same person as I had seen the day before. *Where is the complacent, thoughtful Dad that I knew and loved? Would he come back?*

With all of us finished with our food, besides the one looking vaguely like my father, my brother continued to rationalize with him. Pretty soon, Mom had the doctor on the line.

I always knew Dad was going to a doctor. I never knew what for.

I had never seen anything like that day that we sat down for dinner, with the light of the setting sun coming into the windows next to our dining room table. And now, the ominous doctor was speaking on the line. The one I had heard about but had never talked to. I wondered what he was saying to Mom. I was shocked. Seventeen-year-old emotions took hold. Confusion. Fear. Questioning. Distrust.

Mom talked to the doctor, explaining what was happening. She didn't cower, try to protect the conversation, or go in the other room as she usually did. We never asked too many questions about the doctor. This was the thing that we let go and didn't push too hard to know the answers to because Mom or Dad would get upset. My questions were diverted when they said, "Oh, we'll talk about that later" or "Do you have to bring that up now, Jenny?" Like there was something wrong with asking. I eventually stopped bringing it up because we never talked about it. This phone conversation, one-sided as it was, was private. *We shouldn't be here for it.* Yet we were.

"He's not eating. He says he has a mission from God and that it's not important anymore." She didn't express more. She kept it simple; maybe so she didn't lose it. Maybe she was like me in that she took action first and felt it later.

My emotions flaring, Mom had a calmness about her. That hadn't been the case a couple of days ago. They both brushed off the other interaction, but I distinctly remember how Mom reacted when Dad said, "I know the Antichrist's name."

We were in the kitchen. She was hungry, again in a rush to put dinner on the table. I didn't see exactly what she did because I was helping take full water glasses into the other room when Dad whispered the name into her ear. I came back in quickly, hoping to overhear. I asked what he said.

"Nothing. Go ahead and get started," she fake smiled as she bolted from the room. My brother, Dad, and I sat down in the dining room without a word. I can only imagine what she did in the bathroom right then. *Was she upset with herself? Was she scared like I was now? Was she laughing about the reality of what just happened and that her husband would say something like that?* The emotion was obvious when we saw tear streaks of mascara smeared out of the corner of her eyes, face blotchy and eyes red when she came back down. Fear in her face as she tried to cover it up.

I looked at the mom in front of us now. Now, she wasn't like that. No fear in her eyes. She took charge, watching me, her son, and her husband's preoccupancy with his mission. She didn't care that she was on the phone with someone who had so much influence on our lives. She didn't care what we heard. She knew she couldn't deny it anymore.

Tilting her head to the side, she said, "I don't know whether he'll talk to you. Okay, okay. I'll ask."

"Will you talk to Dr. Wilson?"

Dad slyly smiled again, that weird, giddy grin that I hadn't seen my father do unless he was trying to be funny. It didn't fit the context. *Dad, stop it! Stop being so weird. Stop NOT making any sense! You're confusing me.*

"What good will it do?" Dad said with an eye roll. Mom glared at him again. He grabbed the phone and said hello. The doctor must have posed a couple of questions, but I was sidetracked. I wondered who this doctor was and what he did exactly. I made up in my mind what he was asking on the other line with Dad's brief responses or murmurs. *What is it about today that made Dad feel this strongly about eating soup? Will it be just for today?* My analysis continued until I finally saw a look of resignation on Dad's face.

"Okay. Okay. Yes, that makes sense. Okay."

Mom looked hopeful and asked, "We're going to the hospital then?"

Dad nodded. "Yeah, but it's not gonna do any good." Discrediting it may have made him feel better. Mom didn't respond. She just put on her shoes, grabbed a jacket, and went towards the door, and came back to guide Dad into the car as Dan and I watched.

Emotions glazed over my face. *Hospital? What would the hospital do?* I was overwhelmed. *Which emotion is it?* I used "I'm tired" for every emotion, usually. That was a good excuse to become emotional, right? *Was I trapped? Uncomfortable? Worried?* I had never seen Dad go to the hospital if it didn't involve blood or aches.

Dad used to be the one to take us to the doctor for earaches, headaches, broken arms, colds, or burns. *For something like this, what kind of treatment is available when Dad has a "mission?"* I came up with question after question in my head as I began to realize that Dad was going to the hospital for going crazy.

They had kept a good secret, Mom and Dad. They really had. And now, my mind was blown. I had no idea what to do with it. When they left, I'm sure Mom turned to Dan to make sure he took care of me. He had to make sure I didn't lose it. All I remember is walking down to my basement room and calling my sister, sobbing.

Lauren could barely make out the words I said as I explained that Dad had gone to the hospital. That he was going crazy, questioning everything that he believed in and why he should even eat. I told her how scared I was. I couldn't process any more. I had reached a breaking point. All I could do was cry.

I couldn't consider any other perspective. I could barely consider my own. I couldn't imagine what it was like for Mom as she left Dad in the hospital that night. I couldn't imagine if he continued to fight, verbally, with Mom in the car and the staff once they arrived. I couldn't imagine what it was like for my sister to receive a call where she was begged to come home. I couldn't imagine what my brother thought about the nonsense that came out of my father's mouth.

Deadlocked, confused, exhausted by all of the crying, I was stuck.

I set my head down on my pillow that night, after writing in my journal as I did most nights, praying. A scared prayer to my Lord and Savior.

> *Father, I ask you to be with my earthly father. Keep him safe... I was scared. I thought he was gonna end his life. Lord, but you are in control. Thank you for being there today. Thank you for being here. I hear you. I heart my brother for being so strong. My mom has so much courage. I look at Mom totally different because of today. She is so strong; you have made her strong. Thank you.*

Gracious, like a good Christian girl, I gathered my thoughts, and I thanked my Savior for what had actually been achieved that night. I saw who my mom was for my dad and what this doctor did for my dad, all in the same moment.

And I was scared beyond belief.

I couldn't trust what was happening around me. Although now written and expressed, I couldn't stop the tears waterfalling down my face. The dam released, as I cried myself to sleep that night. I wished, hoped, and prayed that Dad would be okay, that Dad would come back, that the doctors would help him. All I could think about was whether Dad would survive the night in the hospital. I had no idea what would or could happen next.

I see this now as a turning point. How this moment, this day, this event would indeed shape my future. And it was only the beginning.

Once I was aware, I could never turn back.

CHAPTER TWO

The Next Day

I WENT TO SCHOOL THE NEXT DAY.

I was extremely busy with my normal junior-year high school stuff: advanced classes, track practice, responsibilities as a church youth leader, everything.

I craved the normalcy of it all. I wanted a Monday morning and a normal day. I was worried about Mom, Dad, and everyone, but mostly I wanted this all to go away for me. I wanted to trick myself into believing that everything was okay. Truly, I didn't want to think about anything related to Dad or the hospital.

Going through my morning routine, Mom showed up at my bedroom door, cordless phone in her hand.

"He wants to talk to you, Jen." I looked at the phone like it was crazy. It was a reminder that Dad wasn't upstairs getting ready for work. When I didn't grab it right away, she prodded, "Do you want to talk to him?"

I nodded. I guessed I did. I didn't know. My body responded before I could think. *Why is my life unstable?* Putting the headset to my ear, I took a deep breath, hesitated, then said, "Hello?"

I wondered if I was still dreaming. Maybe he wouldn't respond. I waited longer. I knew already that he still wasn't okay. Not like I expected him to be okay yet, but I was hoping, praying, *wishing* that he would be.

"Hi, how are you?" the daze clearly in his voice. The same state I saw in his eyes yesterday showed up in his voice now. It was spacey, sounding more like me than Dad. Just like the questioning from the day before. That was more like me. And, I could get away with it. I was fun, smart, blond-ish, spacey, and in high school. This wasn't Dad. Sometimes he would forget things, and he would call us by the wrong names, but that was a normal dad thing to forget, right? This phone call was like he was living in another world and speaking into one of those telephone games at the playground. I could kind of hear him, but the tunnel made it muffled. Maybe it was due to my own sense of feeling overwhelmed. I processed all of this in literally a second of talking with him. I could hear it as he said hello. He wasn't there.

"I'm okay," I said, lying through my teeth. I was used to not telling the truth about my emotions. I usually stuffed them down, eventually getting mad at them and myself, then they all blew up at the same time. That's all I could manage. I definitely wasn't okay.

"How are you?" I asked him. I didn't know whether he was coherent enough to respond to the question. *Are we going to pretend like we're all okay even when we aren't, again? Let's forget that this ever happened. Let's deny that anything happened, or that anyone is upset. There's no reason to be upset, right? I'm overreacting again. That must be it, right?* I was trying so hard for that.

I couldn't muster up any more fakeness. This whole thing was unprecedented. The clarity in Dad's voice, his intelligence, and his practicality were gone. He hesitated again. I thought maybe he didn't hear the question. It was simple. It was normal. *Should I say it again?* Silence on the other end. Unsure of what to do while I waited. Dad finally responded, "Jen, I'm scared."

Dad's scared? No way. He was the one who scared the boogeyman out of the closet for me. He had encouraged me when I was terrified of performing a skit in the eighth-grade variety show. He was never scared that I knew of.

I had an opportunity to support and love my dad in a time of his life that he needed it. And I couldn't. Those few words were all I could handle. *He can't be the one that tells me how he is feeling. I've been scared. I am scared. I've always been the one who needs support. Now that it's flipped, what does Dad want from me? What do I say now?*

There was a longer pause. I didn't have anything else to say. *Why wasn't he saying anything? How did he have access to a phone?* Unimportant questions came into my space, and I didn't have the words to say them. I didn't know what to do. That fear that I sobbed out the night before came back up. I didn't want to cry anymore. I didn't want to cry right before going to school. Mad at the tear falling down my face, I wiped it away. Now I was mad. *How could he make me cry right now? Why am I letting him get to me?*

I hoped that Mom wouldn't notice when I handed her back the phone. She was close, standing just outside my room in the hallway. Maybe she wanted to support me and check if I was okay? I'm sure she wondered how Dad was and what he would say.

The pause continued. I had to go. *Why did he call if he had nothing to say?* Another tear slipped out of the corner of my eye. Frustrated. Mad. Sad. Annoyed. School was starting soon. I had to go pick up my friend and her sister down the street. I had deadlines and tests. I had to take my brother. I had responsibilities. I had friends to look out for. I had running to do. I couldn't just sit and wait on the phone for something to happen. I had to fill my time. I had to make myself busy, so I didn't have to feel this. I didn't want to think about this. *Maybe if I stuff it down, it will work this time?* That had been one of my strategies in times of trouble.

My eyes filled up again, impatient with anger this time. These emotions shouldn't be happening right now. In fact, they should never happen. They aren't okay. They can't be here now. Everyone can read my upset on my face. Embarrassing. I'm not crying today. I'm not doing that. I'm not talking to my dad on the phone anymore. I'd made up my mind.

I sighed aloud, an indication of letting go of emotions for me, then I said, "Well Dad, I… uhh… I gotta go. School and stuff."

Normal high schooler response. *Doesn't Dad know he called me? Doesn't he realize that I have things to do with my day? Doesn't he want to wish me a good day versus just stay on the line and not say anything? Is this the same Dad who made sure we left for school on time? He made me say goodbye? That was weird.*

Maybe he wanted "normal" too. Maybe he wished he was home, going to work, doing the same things he always did. Maybe he just wanted to say hi to his daughter. Maybe he was concerned about how I was reacting. Maybe that's why he was talking to me. Maybe he wanted support, like the time I told my dad when he was crying uncontrollably, "Maybe you don't have to have a reason to cry."

That day wasn't today. After this call, I went exactly where I usually did. My journal. I must have had a bit more time before leaving for school, a couple of minutes at least, because I wrote:

> *It was weird. Thank you for being with him. Allow Mom the sleep she needs.*

I was concerned about Mom and Dad. I was *always* concerned for others before myself. I was also concerned about the fear welling up in me. It was beginning to crush me. I didn't know that I could feel all these things at the same time. I didn't know that confusion, sadness, anger, and fear could meld together into one big conglomerate that would ooze out of my pores throughout the day at school. It was getting bigger as I kept discovering new things about Dad and life. The life I had been a part of and also missed. I had missed this. *How could I have missed this?* Anger. Self-critique. Disoriented. Irritated. Frustrated. Sad.

First, school. Distraction was better than confusion. I could prioritize things I knew to do. I could make it to the next class, the next break. I didn't tell anyone about it. I didn't tell my best friends Gia or Bella. I only talked about what was necessary for my day, nothing else. I lied when people asked how I was. "Okay" for me wasn't really okay. I expected that those who really knew me would read between the lines. I was bad at pretending, but when my brain didn't let me do anything else, I was "fine." I was confused and upset, craving Normal with a capital N. I stayed Normal. I didn't let any of my friends catch it. If they had asked anything, I ignored it or put it aside. *Not today.*

I don't remember if Mom took that day off work. Maybe she went to work to keep up with Normal too. Maybe she needed it. Maybe she needed the time to let herself process. Or maybe she was at the hospital with Dad. It didn't really matter.

After school, after my regular track workout, the track team was given the responsibility of facilitating a middle school track meet until 7:30 p.m. This was more of what I needed after a stressful weekend. Structure. All I had to do was record the middle schoolers' times with a stopwatch. Thank goodness I didn't have to decide anything. This provided me peace or at least obliviousness. Or maybe it was avoidance. Yep, that's how I put it in my journal that night:

> *I just avoided it today... I just lasted thru... I'm so tired.*

Emotionally tired. Physically tired. That word "tired" always gave me the out I needed, so I didn't have to express myself and my emotions. A perfect excuse. No one could bother me if I said I was tired. In a way, it was the truth. Exhausted. Spent. Drained. Depleted.

My sister, Lauren, surprised me at the track that afternoon with Mom. I was obviously busy in my element, and as soon as she knew I saw her, she left with Mom to go home. She had heard me the night before. My immediate thought was that she had only come because I had called and had embarrassingly freaked out. She made it work so she could be there for our family and me. Little did I know that Dad had called her multiple times the day before too. She already knew. She was there for all of us.

Regardless, I thanked God for her recognizing what I needed. Thank God she showed up. She knew even before I did. It seems like she always did.

As busy as the day was, there was still the night to come. I begged Mom to let me go see him. *Lauren was going, why couldn't I?* The look exchanged between my sister and my mother was inexpressible. They knew I couldn't handle it. They knew that I would be affected by another unpredictable moment in time. All in a thirty-hour time frame. I'm sure they wanted to protect me. I wasn't having any of it. *I can handle it.*

I lived for the expected and pretended like I didn't. When things didn't go the way I thought they should, I cried. I sucked at hiding it most of the time, except for my "triumph" at school that day. I wonder if my friends would have agreed. They probably knew something was off. My behavior usually was back-and-forth—enthusiasm and then devastation. I was currently in devastation/panic mode. I hoped that going to see him would solve this. I *had* to see Dad to know for sure.

"Please, Mom? Let me see him. I don't know if I can go through another day..." tears formed. My weakness. I couldn't complete that sentence. I was concerned for him. I wanted to let him know that I was there for him, especially because I hadn't been there for him that morning. I'd been beating myself up all day about how I didn't have anything to say. I *had* to see why he was scared.

My family was concerned if I would be okay. I could see it in their eyes.

I pulled myself together to say this last word, "Please?"

I don't think I bat my eyes like one would expect when trying to get your mother to give in. Sometimes, tears are enough. Mom understood them too. I noticed her tears most when she was mad at Dad, was too frustrated to say anything, or when she was stressed. For me, tears just appeared with no notice. *Are tears my automatic manipulation so I could get what I want?* I was second-guessing their meaning and how malicious I truly was. *I could use them this way too?* Annoyed with myself. Fear. Anger. Sadness. Tears. This time they worked in my favor.

"I don't think they'll let us all in." She had given in or had at least thought about it. It was a win, as much of a win as it can be to go see your Dad in the hospital.

"It's okay. Let me go. We can take turns, we can make it happen," I said. My driven mentality appeared. The belief that anything was possible gave me hope.

"I don't think it works like that," Mom stated clearly.

I waited, not knowing either. I simply looked at her. Maybe my sister said something in my defense. I don't remember. Tick tock, tick tock.

"Well, we only have a little bit more time for visiting hours. We'd better go." Mom consented.

Too consumed with what I might see, I didn't celebrate my "victory." I was too overwhelmed with the fact that my sister had come to see me and too exhausted physically from the track workout and the kids I had monitored. I was too upset by the fatigue accompanied by emotional distress and too devastated by the complexity of my own emotions. I couldn't think straight. I hadn't even showered from running. All I could do was act. So when Mom said go, I went. I hopped in the car.

It was quiet on the drive. My eyes were taking it all in. We were driving to the same hospital that Grandma had been in multiple times when she fell down the stairs. We drove the same route we always did, past Grandma and Grandpa's turnoff, past the emergency room we went to when Dan broke his thumb and his arm. But everything looked different.

Finally, Mom stopped the car, and we walked together into a section of the hospital I'd never seen before. We went through one door and then another labeled "Psychiatrics," and waited to be signed in. Something had changed. *Is it me?* I was seeing my dad in a psych ward. *What exactly is wrong with him?*

Just kidding about that question. I knew what was wrong with him. It just didn't register completely in this circumstance.

Lauren had told us right before she left for college.

"Before I leave, I just want you guys to know, Dad has... bipolar... disorder," she said slowly. My brother and I had no idea what bipolar disorder was. We had no idea of its impact on us or on Dad. Turned out, it wasn't normal. The weird inconsistencies we saw weren't just how someone could be human. He was affected by something outside of himself. Not necessarily all of the time, but at least a couple times a year for weeks at a time. When Lauren said that, neither Dan nor I had anything to say. I had no questions to ask, as I was tongue-tied and shocked. It was beyond reason, but I knew she had to be right.

We always knew something was off, so this explained it. Dad took meds every day, and brought them anywhere we stayed overnight. I'd never looked at them closely. He never let me, nor did I try. Those were the signs. *But what does that really mean?*

She explained how she had done some research, and so could we. She was nineteen and knew more than we did. She offered herself as a resource if we had questions. That was it. At least we knew something now.

Behind the scenes, Lauren had given my parents an ultimatum of sorts. She told me she said, "You should tell them. And, if you don't tell them before I leave for school, I will." What pressure that must have been on herself and on my parents. What devastation that must have been that she felt that she had to do that. She just wanted us to know. She wanted us to be able to make informed decisions about our future. She wanted us to be able to know that Dad wasn't normal all the time and that there was a reason for that. Thank God for her willingness to do something that was hard, even when it was met with disagreement. How much I love her for that.

Now, besides the previous day, this was the first real evidence of a medical diagnosis. Its reality showed up in the waiting room of the psych ward.

I said nothing as we waited. When they said we could have only two people at a time, I didn't say anything. It was getting late. Visiting hours were almost over. Maybe Mom had talked them into letting me go in because I was only seventeen. Maybe she talked them into it because Lauren came in from out of town. *Chicago's out of town from the suburbs, right? Did Mom just lie?* Maybe it was because she knew that I would have bugged her or been even more worried if I didn't see him. Finally, they let the three of us in to see him. We would have only fifteen minutes. They brought us back through that hallway, two at a time, into the room.

He was sitting on a bed with a yellow-brown blanket, wearing sweatpants and a t-shirt. It seemed normal enough. *This is what a psych ward looks like?* I didn't know a place like this existed until today. I looked around, taking it all in.

Lauren interacted with him first, asking a couple of questions.

"Don't worry, Jesus is coming back. You don't have to worry about me," Dad reassured his daughter.

Nothing had changed. He didn't answer what she asked. Maybe I was hoping that seeing him would bring him back to us. What I saw in front of me was merely the symptoms of bipolar disorder at its extreme. It was still the same crazy person that took over my dad. The one that had been there my whole life, waiting to emerge just like this. *Had he been like this before and I hadn't seen it?*

"What's it like here?" I gained the courage to ask something. *Go me!* Achieving. Five short words that kept him speaking.

"It's like hell in here." He paused again, adding, "Dr. Wilson has put me in hell."

The negativity lingered in the air. My concern for him grew tenfold. *Hell?* We were all going to heaven. We were all saved by grace through Jesus Christ. Hell is never a place I would want to go. Nor did I want Dad there.

"And how do you feel?" Lauren asked, ignoring all of the other questions he didn't answer.

"I feel like hell." I'm sure he said more that day. I blocked it out. I couldn't hear anymore. I couldn't keep it in. I wasn't reassured. I

30

wanted Dad to be okay. *Who is this Dad in front of me? Why is he using the word we're not supposed to use?*

Who am I? Where am I? When will I wake up? Tell me this isn't happening. I wrote about this in my prayer journal that night:

> *He's scary. I keep imagining doing things but I don't see him in it and that makes me sad.*

I thought he'd disappeared from our lives. I'd thought he wouldn't be back. He would never be back to normal. *That happens sometimes, right? People don't come back from breakdowns like this, right? What if this was it?* I thought this was the end of Dad.

I didn't see anything as "bipolar disorder" before now. *What if I can't recognize it again in the future?* Sometimes Dad just acts weird, that's how he is. That's Dad.

> *I want Dad in (the picture) with us—I want him happy and in the family. I don't want him to feel that way... I don't want Dad to feel alone and depressed. We love him and we want to take care of him. Lord, Father, take care of him for me please.*

I begged and pleaded with my Lord. I needed his help. It seemed that I needed everyone's help. I couldn't do anything. I couldn't understand what was happening. I couldn't explain to Dad why he had to eat. I couldn't ask him what was scary about this place. I couldn't express my overwhelmingly significant emotions. I couldn't. Lastly, I prayed for myself. I asked God to do something, so I could sleep.

> *Put my mind at ease.*

Ease. That is not how I would describe the last couple of days. *Give me ease, Lord. Please?*

CHAPTER THREE

My First Mental Health Day

I WASN'T GOING TO SCHOOL TUESDAY. MAYBE.

That was another thing out of the ordinary. You know how some moms let you take a "personal day" when you're not feeling well? You get to bum around the house "just because," or even hang out together during the day? We never did that. My mom never gave permission for us to skip school. It goes to show how my parents valued school. So this was unusual. I felt like I was floundering, as this was uncharted territory. When shy Jenny comes into play, she never asks. She thinks she can handle it all.

The conversation was probably between Mom and Lauren as they analyzed the way I was acting after the hospital. Dad's daze transferred to me as the overwhelm of emotions continued to pile up. All I had avoided during the day came to me. I was tired and all over the place emotionally.

Lauren posed an easy, non-trying question to me like this: "Are you okay?"

Seems like a simple enough question, like you could answer it in a heartbeat, yes or no. For me, I couldn't answer. This person knew me. My sister had been alive my whole life. My sister was three years older than me, four years ahead in school. Although I never saw us as the closest, we got along pretty well. She knew when something was wrong. I knew I couldn't lie to her. I couldn't fake it with my family, although I tried. Everyone knew I didn't admit when I wasn't doing well. They wanted to see if my teenager-turning-into-adult mind could finally make sense of the tears or the overwhelmed haze. I usually cared about everything. Maybe they wanted to know if I could communicate it.

I'm not prone to opening up with more than one person at a time. When it's a one-on-one conversation, I tend to give more feedback, more truths, less pretending, and more "let's get real with Jenny" true input. But I couldn't answer that question. *How could I not answer this?* It's so easy. Yes. No. Two options, clear and simple. Or even, "I don't know" works; I guess that's three options. *Say anything, Jenny. Come on. She's looking at you. She wants you to respond. She wants to know whether you're okay. You know that you're not. You know that something is wrong. You know that you can' t do it right now. You know you need something from someone. You know it. Now just say it. What do you need? Will you let your big sister care for you?* My head spun with this non-complex question that I had turned into something bigger. Sounds like my life.

"Well…"

She could have interrupted me and said, " We know you aren' t! You can' t see it. We know you need a break. Why can' t you say what you need? Why don't you ask for it?" To me, from her question, it was like she was yelling at me to understand myself. She wanted me to know who I was and how to take care of myself. In reality, none of that actually happened.

She could have been pissed off and said, " Aww, forget it. I don't know why I even came out here. You were worried about nothing. Dad will be fine—this is just a cycle. Didn't you do any research when I told you last year? This is common. This is what could happen with someone who has bipolar disorder. Duh." But she didn't. She could have been frustrated at my delay. The same way I was frustrated at Dad's hesitation from earlier that day. That seemed like a year ago now. Had it really only been thirty-two hours since Dad was admitted into the hospital?

All I could muster up was the next sentence.

"I'm scared... and I..." gasp in the middle, of course, as I broke down, "don't... know what to do." Tears. I was worried that talking would lead to uncontrollable sobbing. I couldn't do that now. Even with my mom and sister, I didn't feel safe to share. Everything I knew had turned upside down. I had no idea that this would shake me the way it had. They could see it, and I could barely say a full sentence.

"Yeah." She pulled me in and gave me a hug. "I know." She knew. She only wanted me to see it for myself. She loved me.

"Jen, how about you come to the city with me tomorrow?" She glanced at Mom to double-check that it was okay. Or they had talked about it already? Either way, they were waiting for my response.

I knew I could handle my school schedule. I could tell my sister what I was up to and why it wouldn't work. Mom would never let me. I had the Sectionals track meet on Friday, and I couldn't skip track practice. I had people to pick up and things to do. Excuses.

And what about my brother? It was like he was immune to everything. I had written in my journal, questioning:

> *Is it you that keeps him strong or is it because he keeps it all inside?*

I tried to figure out what super skill I was missing that somehow my brother had inherited. *How does he let go of things? Maybe it had to do with his undying faith?* That's the only thing that made sense to me. *Why did I have to feel so intensely? How come I couldn't let this go? Why wasn't I better at that?* I immediately focused on my flaws. *I am so good at getting mad at myself. I get upset at my emotions. Why can't I be like everyone else? Why can't I be the leader I had always admired in my sister? Why can't I have the even-keeled mentality of my brother?*

Maybe he debated like I did about keeping everything in. Maybe he didn't have the words to say anything. Maybe he didn't know what he was feeling. Maybe it wasn't important to him. Or maybe he dealt with everything in a different way. *Why can't I do better? Why can't I do it "right?"* I went into the normal, the safe, the expected, brushing aside the existential questions when I finally said, "Well, I have a lot of stuff to do, running and school and everything." *Eloquently said.* It seemed like I would never have the words to say what I need to say. I could never say what I was actually thinking.

"Yeah, but people take days off all of the time. What's one day?" Lauren said. "And, you can run in Chicago, or you can come back in time for practice. I have things to do too, but you could just relax for the day. After all that has happened, you deserve it."

She didn't have to say that this was hard on everyone. I couldn't see it because I was too focused on me. Thank goodness she didn't say I was a mess. I would have gotten defensive. I would have been upset that she was "accusing me" of something that was actually true. I probably wouldn't have taken the day off to "prove" that I could do it. And, as many times as my sister had messed up in being there for me, as all sisters (and people) do, this wasn't one of them.

My seventeen-year-old self brought on the drama that my sister didn't like me. I couldn't understand how Lauren was so serious and how she wouldn't be silly with me. I couldn't understand how high school or college was for her.

In my eyes, she had it all. She had close friends, was busy, popular in our church group, and a leader. There couldn't have been anything wrong with her life. Her responses to what I did never made any sense to me. *Why is she upset about the fact that I talk and sing in the morning? Why is she upset that I get so silly with my friends? Why wouldn't she be my friend?* I wanted her to be closer to me, and yet, I felt left out. She had her people, and she didn't need me. And, she still was my sister. When she was gone, I truly missed her.

She knew I was in over my head this time. Maybe she wanted to be there for me. Maybe she knew I didn't know how to express myself either. Somehow, I felt like she just knew.

It seems like Lauren was always there for me when I needed it most. This was one of those times. I see now how countless times, when I can't express myself, she knows. This intuition I've always been fighting, I see my sister listen to hers. And she knew what to do. She knew how to be there for her little sister.

So I said yes.

That next morning, I slept the whole drive to Chicago.

She dropped me off alone in her dorm, set me up with a laptop, and a movie that she loved.

"You've never seen it? You should watch it."

So I laid around in her bed, taking in where I might be in a couple of years. What freedom I had looking at my watch and it said 9:20 a.m., and I wasn't in school. My haze led me first to my writing, where I always go. I prayed through writing as I always did:

> *Our plan is working. It's magnificent.*
>
> *I pray that [Gia] has a good day, and that she finds people to walk with to classes. Be with Daddy—straighten out his head—let him think clearly. Let him be safe with himself.*
>
> *I realize now that prayers should not be*

emergency based. It should be all the time. Continuous. We shouldn't have 9-1-1 prayers. Lord, I ask that you give me the prayer life that will be pleasing to your sight.

It's hard b/c every time I think about my dad and his being bipolar—I think that when I was born, that's when it happened, but it's not true. It's not my fault. Satan's trying to convince me that Dad being sick is my fault, but I know it's not. You're allowing all of this to happen and you know what is going on. You are helping him in what you are supposed to.

You promise me: Isaiah 49:15 "Can a woman forget her nursing child, that she should have no compassion on the son of her womb! Even those may forget yet I will not forget you." Thank you for not forgetting me—ever! And not forgetting Dad either. You remember us always. Thank you.

Getting my thoughts on paper was a release. It was a way to connect with God. I wasn't doing 9-1-1 prayers (only calling on Him in an emergency), but I was ragging on myself as if I were. I was always hardest on myself, giving myself the "shoulds" when all I needed to do was to let myself be there for me. Let others be there for me. Let God be there for me. Let Him know the desires of my heart. I took comfort in my faith and writing. This was my process. I wasn't doing any of the normal today. No one would interrupt me, no one would get in my way, so I could do whatever I wanted.

After finishing my writing prayer, I distracted myself the best way I knew how.

Lauren had warned me the movie *Finding Neverland* would be sad. I cried with it. Even though I'd been crying the last couple of days, it was acceptable here. Alone, I could simply wipe the tears away and move on.

Nothing else stood out for me about what Lauren and I talked about that day. It was good to be in a setting unconnected to my home and get my mind off things. Even the train ride back to the suburbs allowed me to break up and process what had happened. I usually had a hard time sleeping, so this "resting" thing was hard for me. I didn't recognize when I needed to do it. I didn't take responsibility for it. The only other thing I did after the movie was sleep.

This "ditch" day was essential to my well-being. I had given myself a break for my own personal mental health. I didn't have to do anything. I didn't have to feel anything I didn't want to. I didn't even have to talk to my sister.

I trusted myself that I wouldn't get in my own way. I came around to trusting myself about not doing a workout that day either. Sometimes, you just need to stop.

Taking a break here was the first time I'd thought about how I might need to do that occasionally. A girl with all the feels. A girl who overanalyzed and tried to make sense out of everything. *Jen, cut yourself a break. Stop taking everything so seriously.*

I kept up the intention to be normal from then on. Pretending had worked for me before, but everything wasn't normal. The way Dad was acting was not normal. Even this day off wasn't normal.

I couldn't ignore my emotions anymore. I had to face them head on. The confusion. The upset. The crying. The emotional intelligence I had gained perhaps was due to my interactions in childhood. I had an ability to see, feel, and express differently than others. I had always been able to tell when someone was upset and comfort them or be with them. I could recognize their emotion even if I couldn't express my own. This was the beginning of noticing it. This extreme upset that I couldn't control was the beginning of being okay with having emotions in general. I was simply grasping for that truth, finally taking time for myself.

All of these emotions had built up, and it was finally time to express them. This was it.

CHAPTER FOUR

My New Normal: Moving Forward

I WENT ON WITH MY WEEK, JUST LIKE I SAID I WOULD, not worrying about anything except my own responsibilities, still shoving the emotions under the rug as best I could. Nothing was in my way. I didn't let it get in my way. Sectionals for track were that Friday. I had school. I had friends. I had responsibilities. I focused on those.

Dad got out of the hospital before Sectionals that Friday. I learned later that it took effort to have him approved to leave by then. Dr. Wilson had pulled together his resources, and Mom fought hard to show how he would be okay and have the support he needed. We couldn't afford any more hospital bills. Dad even said that he wasn't completely well that Friday afternoon, and he came to my meet.

We warmed up as usual at our home track for the 4x800 meter race, the first event of the competition. I barely talked about anything. Sensitive and quiet, I kept these events of the past week to myself. Our family secret. I think my family liked it that way. I didn't have the words to say either. So it worked for me. I hadn't delved into what bipolar disorder was, researched, or taken any new actions except on Tuesday by taking the day off. I hadn't journaled or prayed about it since that day either. I was at school—I was running—I was where I needed to be. Dad wasn't home at night—

that was the only difference. It was nice to forget by keeping busy. Until I couldn't anymore.

My track team qualified for State in the 4x800, automatically getting us to the Illinois State High School Track Meet. This year was more exciting than the others. The previous years, I had gone as an alternate. This time I would be racing on race day. A dream come true!

After running the 1600-meter race and not qualifying as expected, I warmed up for the final event at the end of the meet, the 4x400. I wasn't as good at the 400-meter race as other distances, so I wasn't worried. My team was the B team, so we only hoped that we could push our other teammates to qualify for the state meet.

I remember seeing Dad for the first time in a week. He was walking around in a circle, pacing, at the back corner of the track. Just like I could tell over the phone by his voice, I knew he still wasn't okay by watching him. My heart sank. Our win from the 4x800 couldn't help me forget this.

Dad could be pretty friendly with my teammates' parents, as we had all run together for a couple of years. And yet, there he was, by himself, not where the other families were at the bleachers, not cheering like he normally was. And no smiling face. He was not talking or interacting. I didn't see Mom either. Dad waited there, alone, pacing back-and-forth, back-and-forth. I was warming up by myself, so I ran over to talk to him briefly.

"Hi, Dad!" I said loudly, out of breath. "Did you see us?"

I was referring to our 4x800. I was hoping. Looking at him in the eyes (or trying to), I knew that he probably wasn't there.

"Yeah." He gazed into the distance, and I couldn't tell if he was going to move around or not. He wasn't comfortable. He wasn't safe yet. He wasn't Dad. He was still allowing the disease to control him. Or maybe the right way to say it is that the disease took hold of him? Maybe I should say it simply: he wasn't better.

Dad told me later how he felt, "I remember distinctly walking around the track because I couldn't keep still and was still quite sick." I knew it. It was obvious. At times Dad would become really excited and talk a mile a minute, and then would resort to his more reserved self. This was different from both of those, different from the normal ups and downs that we naturally have. I couldn't identify this at the time. I thought what was in front of me was a nervousness that someone would find out. This was uncomfortable. This was uncertainty. Dad told me later that "restless feet," or akathisia (what I called pacing) is a well-documented side effect of Zyprexa, an antipsychotic that had been used to treat his episode. Turns out, he was walking because of the treatment of his condition, not because of bipolar disorder.

Either way, there wasn't anything I could do. He still wasn't fully back, to me.

◆ ◆ ◆ ◆ ◆

Going to the State Track Meet again was exhilarating, and there were so many things to prepare. I grew up in that moment, standing on the side of the track before my race, recognizing which Dad I had in front of me.

This is the one who, in my eyes, still had mania. I wouldn't have been able to call it that, but I knew it deep down. I was still worried about him, for sure. But it was no longer all-encompassing. He was out of the hospital.

I had my own life to think about, so I focused on that. I had to think of myself. I had to do my race. I had to keep doing the things I wanted to do, and Dad could take care of himself. He had to. I couldn't take on any more responsibility regarding it. I put this Dad thing aside. I created my life to be busy, full of activities and events. I kept doing the things I had done every year, with the pressure of performing and achieving in track on my shoulders.

That next week, the state track meet was the most epic meet of my life. I not only ran my own personal record the second week in a row, but as I handed off the baton, I watched my teammates move their way forward in the pack. I had the opportunity to watch my team, my girls, my friends, pull into the front and beat the 4x800 Illinois state record by six full seconds! 2:18, 2:17, 2:16, 2:15, each individual 800-meter time passed the finish line with one second less.

I never beat that time again in my running career in spite of running competitively for four more years. That day was one of the best days of my life. Dad told me later he almost didn't come home due to being sick. If he hadn't been there, I would have been devastated. He chose to come, even though he knew it would be hard for him and my mom amongst people he didn't want to know about this.

◆ ◆ ◆ ◆ ◆

We were getting Dad back slowly but surely. I wasn't questioning what was happening anymore. There was enough stability, enough structure. I was okay. There was enough of Dad's private, inquisitive personality, and his random outbursts, that I didn't notice the disease the rest of the school year. And I had just won the state meet. I mean, what more could you want as a seventeen year old? Being a track star and breaking records became my identity. The rest simply faded away.

Sadly, I didn't notice the things Mom had to deal with when I wasn't around; the things that I didn't recognize and the things that maybe she couldn't explain either. Dad slept all the time in recovery, while Mom picked up the slack around the house. This was the normal bipolar outside of the upset, the one I hadn't discovered for myself, and the one I still couldn't really see most of the time.

The story continues. This episode was over for me. Although it continued for a couple more weeks (at the very least), the impact wasn't as huge as it was the first day and first week that Dad went into the psych ward. I continued with the busyness of my life.

When my mission trip happened in Idaho, I emotionally exploded. Grandpa (Dad's dad) had just gone into the hospital. Turned out, he had a stroke when he was in Nigeria. I was worried about my family. Worried about my mom, worried about Dad, worried about me. *What would happen to Dad if something else happened to Grandpa? Would he fall into another episode? What if I wasn't there? Would they tell me?* I saw more and more how the mix of my own emotions didn't give me time to be present with the people serving on the mission trip with me. I didn't allow myself to be vulnerable with them and learn from them. Fear. Upset. Frustration. *Why was I here?*

My bottled-up energy, and the influence of frustration, grief, and anger came out on the last day. It was our outing day, so we went on a hike and explored. I had tears streaming down my face practically the whole time.

I had trusted one guy with information about my dad, and I was angry at him because he never followed up with me the entire two weeks we were there. Granted, I never asked him to, but I had expected him to reach out to see how I was doing. I cried and told him my expectations and how he didn't fulfill them. I had wanted him as my friend, especially because he knew my family.

The rest of my feelings emerged as I confronted others one by one. Left out. Betrayed. Questioning. All the emotions. Tears. Apologies exchanged. Expectations expressed. Hindsight allows me to see how I always expect people to follow up with me. *Why didn't they automatically? Couldn't they tell that I was feeling left out? They must not be smart enough*. Distrusting. Sensitive. Upset. Abandoned. Tired. Expectant. I thought these people were my friends. They were, but I didn't see it like that when I brought it up. I only saw the betrayal, the upset, the overwhelm of emotions that I had.

Denying that I was sensitive, I didn't see how affected I was from the previous school year. I didn't see how impacted I had been throughout my life by seemingly little things. How emotional I was about everything. Not just Dad's breakdown, but everything. The ups and downs were normal, and yet, maybe not.

As I moved into my senior year, I only saw snippets of worry that would emerge in my prayer journal. In September of my senior year, I wrote:

> Daddy's been acting really weird, trying to be funny when he's not and then going to bed early—I don't know which one he is now. I just don't know what is going on. And I wish Mom and Dad would just tell me what was going on instead of just letting me guess. Cuz I worry too much. I'm worried that Dad will be crazy again— because I can't handle that. I really can't, Lord. The only way I could handle it would be if you gave me strength.

I still believed in God, but still distrusted my family. Perhaps I was feeling powerless? Worried. Upset. Weird. Definitely uncertain.

I thought that they would know which side of the spectrum, mania or depression, Dad was leaning to. I didn't realize that they were both probably questioning the same thing, just at a deeper level. Should we adjust his meds? Is he okay? Will he have to be hospitalized again? What should we do, Dr. Wilson? Or is it too soon to tell?

And then I was off to senior year, where I was asked to homecoming, had a boyfriend for the first time, and truly enjoyed my sexless, non-drinking senior year of track and cross-country, good friends, and good times. I made major life decisions for me, not attending the church missions trip that next summer, deciding to go to Illinois State University, the state school (instead of the Christian ones I applied to), and the whirlwind of senior year whizzed past.

Dad got lost at my graduation, perhaps as a result of unrecognizable (to me) mania or depression? Hard to know, maybe it was just Dad being Dad. It was all a blur but felt like nothing new, nothing extreme or completely unusual.

So I continued my life. All the emotions were the same. Sometimes I would worry, but mostly I was ready for the next steps. Overanalyzing. Uncertain. Ups. Downs. Graduating and moving forward.

I was focused on me and what I was to become.

❖ ❖ ❖ ❖ ❖

College came and went. Drinking underage rarely happened, as I would always be kicked out of a party by the police before it started. Since police frequently broke up parties, it had killed my own vibe to join in the drinking. I never wanted to lose control, always thought I needed to keep it together. Otherwise, who knew what people would discover or what I would discover. With Christianity still as one of my main tenets, I judged people for drinking and didn't understand why people did it so intensely.

Still wanting to be accepted, I would joke with people, telling them I was bad luck, when in reality, I didn't care if I was drinking or not. I could have fun without it. But due to the trend of college and new drinking buddies, I started to believe that I couldn't connect with people unless I drank. Twenty-one was a phase where everyone wanted to see me drunk because of not participating in the past. After a night of dancing with one group of people, the rest of my twenty-first birthday led to me crying with self-created drunken pressure; too much expectation of myself. I blamed it on my friends. Not fun. All of the emotions came up in the drunk, uncomfortable fashion that we're all familiar with. Upset. Anger. Left out. Betrayal. Besides, I didn't trust anyone to take care of me, not my friends, definitely not myself. *Where are those real friends again?*

I didn't realize that people are humans and make mistakes. Sometimes you get mad at the close friends you have, just like family. That type of anger wasn't okay to me. I didn't see how the pressure I put on myself was diminishing the joy and fun I could have in life. The overachiever in me watched my stress levels increase my junior year as I continued on the path to do a five-year teaching program in four years. I did it to save money and organized my classes strategically. I also tried to be there for my family so that my brother wouldn't have to take out as many loans as I did. I wanted the whole family to be okay. In my senior year of college, I did my student teaching in Chicago, as I had always wanted. It was my dream.

When I got to student teaching, all I started to feel were the responsibilities at the level of an adult. It wasn't fun, and I didn't know I wasn't ready. I didn't know what to do, and I was mad, sad, and frustrated all at the same time. During that year, I found out so much more than I ever expected.

My biggest question was: *Do I really have to be an adult?*

At that point, I didn't want to.

CHAPTER FIVE

Depression: When I Understood It

I'D NEVER FELT LIKE THIS BEFORE. I really hadn't. In my senior year of college now, reality and expectation were far off. I didn't know what had come over me. After all, I've had a pretty decent life, no reason to be upset. No reason to be depressed. Critique. Critique. Critique. I was hard on myself before I could let myself feel. I didn't know that I didn't know what people were talking about when they mentioned depression. I didn't know what my dad had gone through, or my friends, or my best friend's sister.

Until that one morning.

It came out of nowhere. In hindsight, I see it was building up to this. My life as it was led up to this morning.

I woke up. I turned over to check the clock. It was a Sunday. I can't remember whether I had been drinking the night before. It doesn't matter. Papers were scattered across my room, begging to be organized, and clothes thrown over the chair, underneath the hanger area in the closet, and the dirty laundry bin untouched in what little extra space was there. It wasn't a big room. I shared an apartment with two other student teachers, each with our own bedrooms. My room was a good size and could easily fit all of the stuff I had. I see now that I didn't know how to put it together as I struggled through student teaching stresses and woes. Organization wasn't my strong suit and still isn't. And, I hated myself for not being organized. In fact, I had started hating myself for everything I did. Nothing was ever good enough. As I look back, I can identify it. At the time, all that came out was self-critique.

Why can't you do this Jenny? What is wrong with you?

I woke up and saw that clock. My normal self would get up and start my day. I used to be that annoying one who would pop up like a daisy without stopping. No wonder my sister was always annoyed. But, ever since I moved from the college campus in Normal and started doing college here in Chicago, practicing adulthood, each day was harder to get up. Each day was not what I wanted it to be. The first semester we had taken college classes and then gone into elementary school classrooms where we observed and taught a couple of lessons. I was seeing my Spanish skills weren't as good as I wanted them to be. Considering I was studying bilingual elementary education, that was important. And yet, I was still motivated. It was on my birthday that year, in September, I remember meeting up with my sister and crying my butt off after only a month of student teaching, only a month with this teacher, Lupe, who was incredible. Except for this moment.

Lupe was hard. She didn't let anything slide with the kids, and she was extremely straightforward with me. For me, she was the stereotype of a Latina who held nothing back. So when I wasn't ready for the lesson that I was to teach on my birthday, she called me out. She told me I needed to revamp my whole lesson, a second-grade science lesson about superficie (surface tension). She told me to get serious. I left school crying, feeling overwhelmed. My sister had already offered to come meet with me for my birthday in Little Village, where I lived. We went to a taqueria and bought tacos. I couldn't stop crying when she asked me how student teaching was going.

"I don't know what to do. I'm trying... my hardest...," tears prevented me from completing my sentence. I couldn't. I had held it together until she asked this question. It's no wonder I hated when people asked me questions. I used to write about how extended family was so annoying because everyone asked me questions at get-togethers. And they wanted answers like hounds finding the scent, like vultures swarming in over the dead carcass. They weren't going to stop without getting an answer. That was my perspective. It couldn't be that they cared about me and were asking about things that I said I was up to. It couldn't be that they were trying to let me share with them about my experience, about my life, about what student teaching and college were actually like for me. Maybe they actually wanted to know. I just didn't want to cry in front of them, again.

I was disappointed in myself because usually, I didn't finish anything. I couldn't see what I had achieved, pulling myself back down into the depths of the downward spiral. Sometimes, I knew I was going there, but I didn't know how to stop it. I only knew how to cry. Tears prevented me from completing my sentences, so I started avoiding people at all costs. I would never be who I thought I would be. I couldn't see the high honors, the division I athletics scholarship, or the nonnative Spanish skills flourishing. I could only see the negative. People would ask, and I would have to admit my failure or dislike of where I was. I kept these thoughts in my head, only judging myself for who I was and what I wasn't doing.

Tears would fall in my way. Every time they happened, I critiqued myself automatically. *You're so weak. You're a loser. You can't do anything. You can't even keep it together to answer a simple question.* My life always sucked. I couldn't be happy. *I won't be happy, and it's not okay. I'm not okay.* This student teaching thing is not okay. *Why am I even doing this? Should I just give up?*

And I'm so behind. I'm always behind. I have never experienced anything. I barely drank. I didn't trust anyone to take care of me. I hadn't had sex, never even masturbated. I hadn't even been kissed at this point. Even with my boyfriend in high school, I broke it off within four months, scared that someone would actually like me. I had been too scared to try anything, afraid it would be "bad" in the eyes of myself, my family, and God. My sister's voice ran in my head when she said, "Don't kiss anyone until you really like them." She had warned me from her high school perspective, and I took it seriously.

All of this was wearing on me. At twenty-two, I wondered, *What have I been up to? Shouldn't I be okay sharing about myself?* I put on this face of "everything's okay." *What if I admitted any of this to my fellow student teachers? They would laugh at me. They would make fun of me. They wouldn't understand.* I felt like no one could ever understand.

I had built up this world of expectation around myself. I had to stay in the box. I had to be someone who everyone expected me to be. I couldn't be me. It was terrorizing me. My own standard of perfection, this version of Christianity I was breaking out of during this year of isolation. I couldn't do anything about it. It was spiraling out of control. I couldn't live up to it anymore. I couldn't reach my goals.

I didn't know how to ask for help or even that I needed help. I couldn't see what to do and wasn't aware of what I was looking for. This unsettling environment, this newness I thought I always wanted—it wasn't what it was cracked up to be. I was worried about making a mistake, caused tension and stress for myself, and spent hours attempting to "fix" it within my student teaching. I didn't realize that there was nothing to be fixed. I kept striving for the perfection I believed my Savior had asked of me. The only way a Christian could be, making up for all of the "bad" things (sin) natural to humanity. It didn't make sense anymore.

Confused. Uprooted. In transition. Expectant. Stressed. Tense. Anxious.

And today, on my birthday, was exactly the same. *They were wrong, my sister really didn't care about me, and why did I have to talk to anyone? Why was she even asking? Did she want to make me cry? What a jerk! No one cares about me.* That was my perspective.

A couple of days before, in my journal, I had written:

> *Communication & expressing how I actually feel is really hard for me. I feel like I always say things that are in the safe zone of things to say so that I won't get hurt but then, how could that even work? Why do I not trust God enough? Why won't I be satisfied by God? Because I want to be loved by others and if someone cares for You will I be satisfied? I know I'm not going to be satisfied by people but I'd rather see, hear, and experience this.*

The annoyance. The frustration. I couldn't see that I was over critiquing, overanalyzing, overcompensating. It wasn't helping. I wasn't allowing myself to discover anything. Instead, I was hard on myself for wanting to be accepted by other people. I wanted God's approval to be enough at the time, and it wasn't working. Instead of letting myself take in the love and acceptance of my Lord, I was hard on myself, expecting undying and unshakeable faith that made me safe, protected, and at peace. In reality, this wasn't happening.

I couldn't see that this requirement I had made up for myself to be perfect, and to be the perfect Christian was crushing me. I couldn't see that being too safe everywhere was killing me. I wasn't risking, thus I wasn't learning. And devastatingly enough, I didn't trust God. I couldn't ever trust Him enough. And I hated myself even more for that. I'd never be enough. Nothing I did would *ever* be enough. I wanted support from others. I wanted others to be there for me. I wanted to be present with people. The perplexity of my "leave me alone" and "take care of me" mentality was confronted by my sister. She knew exactly what to say to encourage me when I was told to revamp my lesson.

"Jen, you can do this. You've wanted to be here in Chicago, doing this program. I don't know exactly what that teacher said, but you're here to grow, and it sucks it's on your birthday..." (we both laughed... yay for making me smile, Sis!) "and you have a chance to go and show her that you're good enough to be a great teacher."

I don't remember much more of what my sister said to me that day. All I know is that she supported me. I know that she gave me the encouragement I needed. The thing I wanted to hear so that I could move on. She gave me the recommendation to sleep well that night because she knew about tears of exhaustion that could contribute to how I was feeling. She gave me the age-old recommendation to "try my best." I would have said that there isn't anything anyone could say when I was confronted like that. There wasn't anything anyone could do except be there for me. She could be my sister and listen, support, and encourage like sisters do. She was there for me.

I don't remember how I recovered on my birthday except for the fact that I revamped the lesson and taught it the next day. I avoided that teacher the whole time before the lesson when she asked what I had changed to fix it. I hadn't followed instructions completely because I didn't like to, and saw myself as a rebel within the system. I fixed what I could get away with. It was close enough. When Lupe called me out on it, I was confronted. *Did it really matter? Did it really make a difference?* I taught the lesson and learned that I could do it. Not perfectly, but I did it.

Back to this morning. This Sunday, I turned to look at the clock, and for the first time ever, I thought that I shouldn't get up. *What was the point? Does it matter? No one really cares about me. Maybe I should just die. Maybe I should kill myself. No one would really care.*

I hate myself. I have no reason to live. Why would I spend one more second in this world when there is nothing to live for? The flash to all of my faults— how terrible, inexperienced, and upset I was, with no control or emotion or belief in God. I couldn't do it right. *This isn't worth staying here for.*

Then it hit me, it clicked. Not in the "I'm happy about it" sort of way, but in a straight realization way. I realized that this is the moment I had been preparing for. I had never thought to not get up in the morning. I had never thought killing myself was the answer. This is the moment that we thought would happen. The click was realizing that I had never considered suicide before, and I'd been set up to know what to do. It wasn't okay.

I wasn't okay.

Thank God, my sister and I were planning for her wedding that year. Thank God, she asked me to be her maid of honor, and we had to talk about the things that she needed to do for her big day. Thank God that she lived up north and had a car so she could come and see me as I was in the midst of student teaching. Stressed out. Overwhelmed. Teaching in my nonnative language. She would come over, and we'd talk and plan. This was the first time outside of living together as kids that we had hung out. She saw something I didn't. She saw this moment as she had before on my birthday. Out of the blue, she said, "Hey Jen, have you ever thought about talking to someone?"

"Someone? What do you mean?"

"Like a therapist."

I had never talked about that with anyone before. I never really understood what therapy was and why to do it.

Silence brewed. And she let it. She was waiting for my response.

I don't remember what I was talking about. It was probably about how I forgot to pay rent and then had a late charge because of it. My parents had even fronted me the money. They were already paying for my rent, so that's how lucky I was. We had taken out the maximum amount of student loans for my brother and me, and an extra TEACH grant, where I would have to teach in a low-income school for four years after I completed my degree. It was my choice to do that (discouraged by my parents), and I used part of it to go to Guatemala the previous summer to practice my Spanish. I had used it to take extra classes so I could graduate early.

When she asked this weird question, we had never talked about it before. This was a first.

So, I asked her in my most judgmental and accusing voice, "Have *you* done therapy?"

Imagine the judgment, lack of enthusiasm, and the attitude associated with that statement. And the accentuation on the word *you*. Yep, it was all there. She luckily didn't interpret it that way and kindly told me about her experience.

She said, "Yep. When I was in college, I was really struggling with school and taking so many classes at once, and I couldn't concentrate. When I went to therapy, my therapist told me that I had ADHD and that perhaps taking medication could help me focus on schoolwork. I had a hard time completing anything and could only do stuff under a deadline. Even with that, I wouldn't always finish it in time."

I'd never heard her talk about this before. So I questioned her. I was curious what it could be used for. Because I didn't have a problem. I didn't have anything that was upsetting in my life... right?

So I asked, "And, what do you talk about?"

"People can talk about anything. I could talk about life, our family, especially with Mom and Dad, but I think it could help you process what is going on in your life right now. It helped me, and maybe it would help you. And, you're still under Mom and Dad's insurance, so you could probably get some pretty good benefits. How about we look it up?"

I sat there, debating why she was telling me this. *Do I need to get over something in my past?* She was wrong. I was fine. Obviously. I was doing the things that I'd always wanted to do. I had wanted to be a teacher since I was a kid. I wanted to do the yearlong student teaching program in Chicago. I was doing it. This was what I wanted.

But why doesn't it feel like that? Why does it feel like I am setting myself up for a trap? Why does it feel like I'm dying slowly inside, that I am more frustrated than happy? Why do I hate where I am living? Why don't I have the community I thought I would? Why is this so different from college? Why is this so difficult? I can handle it by myself, right? I was doing it. I would spend hours working on my computer at night, planning for the most creative, original lessons for the next day. *I don't need to talk to anyone. Could I even trust a therapist? Why would she suggest that?*

I didn't want to look it up. *Am I not open enough to even look?*

I was judging myself for being scared. What if I couldn't... what if... I asked her the question that I was nervous about.

"But, couldn't Mom and Dad find out that I'm going to therapy?" Scared. Dripping with judgment and critique.

"There's HIPAA laws, Jen."

When I looked at her in confusion, she asked, "You don't know what HIPAA is?"

When I shook my head, eyes darting to the side, embarrassed I didn't know, she explained:

"HIPAA means that you can be protected from any doctor giving out medical personal information, I think once you're over the age of eighteen. Unless you authorize them to have access to your records, they can't look at where you go to therapy. And therapists have confidentiality laws as well. Mom and Dad won't know anything except the name on the account, and even that, you could pay for it, so they wouldn't know."

That was the biggest thing to find out. I didn't want Mom and Dad to know that I was seeing someone and talking about them. At that point, I didn't want anyone knowing what I was actually up to. *Wouldn't that be weird to talk to someone openly about my life and my past?* We'd never talked about therapy as a family. I'm sure Mom and Dad would say I was wasting my money. I didn't want to hear it. Only people who are mentally unstable have to talk to therapists. Lauren opened up to the fact that she talked to one. And she's not like that. She's my sister, but she's not too ridiculous to have extra help by talking to someone. I'd never been exposed to anyone who went to therapy, that I knew of. And if I did, I would judge them right away. *They're weak. They couldn't get their life together. Shouldn't they know how to handle this? Or, they just weren't trusting God enough.* For sure. That must be it. This wasn't in my repertoire. *Besides, there isn't anything broken with me. Is there?*

I was at the point that I knew something wasn't working. I was inside all of the time, nervous about living in a neighborhood that had major crime and gangs everywhere I walked, even though I pretended not to be. It was prevalent; something was happening around me that I couldn't see. The gringa with partial observation skills and lack of complete knowledge of Mexican Spanish, there was no way for me to catch everything. I was getting depressed. *And if Lauren said that therapy worked for her and it wouldn't cost me a lot, and the HIPAA law could prevent Mom and Dad from knowing what I was doing, then, I guess, why not?*

"But... how do you find one?" I asked hesitantly.

"Here... where's your computer? I'll show you. I think Mom and Dad have pretty good insurance..." She looked around, and I closed down all of my tabs before I let her use my computer, sitting on the couch in my Little Village apartment.

We spent some time searching, me asking a ton of questions about how to approach this, and how Lauren approached it. The barrier broken, we connected. She helped me look up various therapists and look at the reviews. It wasn't as hard as I thought. My brain swirled as I was still considering this new idea. There was one doctor who stuck out. Madison Clark. Her therapy looked like it would line up with me. She was someone who could relate to my experiences. That was that. I logged her name and number in my phone and told my sister I would call her sometime. Obviously, that would be if I felt like I needed it. *And I won't.*

Before Lauren left that day, she turned to me as she was walking out the door, "You know, I had to have Lucy (her best friend) call for me. Let me know if you need me to make that call. I'll help you set up the first appointment."

I closed the door on her, thinking that would never happen. Thinking that maybe I'd consider it, but I didn't need it. *Things will work out. They always do. They always have.*

As student teaching continued, I had stopped writing. I was too busy for it. I barely wrote my prayers out anymore. I was beginning to lose the Christian faith that I believed in my whole life. It just didn't make sense to practice it without my religious community back at school. It all started to seem so fake whenever I was at church. The doubting I'd had since thirteen came back, even though I thought I had gotten over it and came back to my faith. I pretended I was okay with it. Then, I was starting off fresh in a new city of Chicago. I stopped keeping track of what I was up to. I made myself busy, too busy to try to make new friends or new communities at church.

Everything had shifted as I became an adult. Impatient. Antsy. Lonely. Frustrated. And utterly alone.

I could do it myself. It was nice of her to offer. But really, what would I need help with? When the time comes, I'll ask for it. Won't I?

I was seeing that trend continue into my teaching style. I had a hard time asking for help. The second-semester student teaching in a second-grade classroom, I was no longer in Lupe's classroom because I had asked to switch; one of the things I regret about my teaching career. When I asked to be transferred after those few months, I didn't realize that I didn't know how to ask for help from Lupe. I felt I couldn't handle her level of critique. I was already criticizing my every move: *Why didn't you see that coming, Jenny? You should have prepared better,* and the worst, *What's wrong with you?* I cried to my supervisor, and she switched me. I never saw the students nor Lupe ever again.

The new teacher had a hard time giving me any feedback except about my nonnative Spanish. I knew I wasn't as good as a native, so that didn't help. Lupe had me crying because she asked me to be fully ready for lessons. That was what I needed. As I became older and further into the teaching profession (and in life), I discovered that I didn't even think to ask someone to help me. I thought I could do it all. I thought I didn't need anyone. It would be hard, but I could do it. By myself.

It took all of the changes: stopping going to church, getting physically attached to my apartment, not having as many friends around, and feeling the complete disconnect from my family that lead to this day.

So I had to make that call to Madison.

That day, by myself, I made a call to a therapist. I know I left a message, floundered, and I'm sure I sounded weird. This call was the one that saved my life. This gave me hope. This made it so that I would live, succeed, and learn to express myself. Because the worst was yet to come. And at least I would live.

I played phone tag when Madison called me back. I guarantee I canceled the first appointment and maybe the second or I completely forgot and didn't show up. Eventually, I showed up at her office. Then it became the only consistent thing I had after I graduated from college with my degree in bilingual elementary education.

I was lucky to have my sister, who set me up for success. I was lucky to have a supportive boyfriend (eventually) who would encourage me to continue to go, and even drive me to my appointments when I was running late.

You could say I was strong because I made the call myself. I don't know if this is true for everyone, but I didn't recognize depression in myself. Honestly, I don't know how I caught it. I only knew I was not myself that morning. Somehow, this triggered my conscious mind to do something that my sister had prepared me for. I am lucky. It took me considering suicide to make the call. I know others don't make it to that.

For me, it took knowing that I had a family that I hated and loved at the same time. My cousin put it best when she said, "You guys love each other, but you don't communicate." Here we had. Here we talked about the hard stuff.

I know the line was somewhat clear for me; for many others it's muddled. This experience is not like everyone else's. I didn't have a suicide attempt because I caught myself. Now I know what it was like. It let me know what it was like to be caught in depression. It gave me the words to speak it. The therapist gave me the words to communicate my emotions. I gained skills that I continue to use daily.

I gained someone who would listen to me, someone who I could admit faults to and was trained to not judge. Although I still judged myself, I had one person to listen. I had trained myself to watch how other people reacted and adapt to what they did. Of course, I did that in therapy too. She gave my words clarity, and through her, I gave my words their voice.

The moment I considered suicide was something that changed my life. I understand more of what people go through to the extent that I can. That is what I am thankful for. I can identify what depression is, and I can respond in a way that will keep me safe. I can trust myself. I finally asked for help.

I finally experienced something my dad did. I finally understand the experience of depression in my own way. What a blessing.

Thank God, I was set up to make that call or perhaps I wouldn't be here. I could have done something that could have ended my life. As low as I was at the time and as low as I have been since then, I now can say what depression looks like for me. I know my faith changed, and yet I'm still extremely grateful for who I believe God is and how He has provided for me. I thank God every day for this and that I experienced this and came through on the other side.

He always provides.

CHAPTER SIX

Could I Have It Too?

"YOU KNOW YOU COULD BE BIPOLAR, RIGHT?" Dad's first words on the phone to me were heart-wrenching that Saturday evening. My worst nightmare.

I stopped dead in my tracks.

My heart sank. I wasn't completely sober. Not drunk, and grateful that I wasn't for this exact conversation. Fear crept into my chest as I considered what my options were, considering my location, and why Dad was doing this now. After twenty-five years of being alive, this was the time?

I was already having a bad night. Self-induced. I never felt included at parties like these, with people I didn't care about, except for my boyfriend. I felt like I wasn't smart enough, not good enough, definitely didn't have enough money, and not stable enough. It was a college-style party, which I had never really fit into, even when I was in college.

Although I wasn't religious anymore, I still felt left out in these experiences. The "left out" part always had me looking for ways to not go to events like these, or leave even though I craved being included. Uncertain. Unsettled. Self-critical.

I wanted an excuse to leave, but I was too stubborn to say it to my boyfriend, and I wanted him to have a fun time. This call was perfect timing, a great excuse. Also, why would Dad call on a Saturday night? So I answered.

I walked down the stairs, away from the noise of the ping-pong balls hitting plastic cups, screaming, and loud music.

"Why do you say that right now, Dad?" I responded at the bottom of the stairs, the winter air blowing at the door, muffling the music slightly. No response.

"Why did you say that?" I repeated, hoping there was a good answer coming from him. Hopefully, a reasonable response or maybe how an unknown test result from high school showed proof. Maybe I was unaware. Maybe I wasn't told. Again.

"I lost my job today." This was the explanation for why he is calling right now. Something happened, something tragic for Mom and Dad, especially Dad. He was a teacher in Chicago, and he had lost his job, again. He was always trying to keep his illness out of his professional and personal life. Discrimination happened consistently, and only recently have people been willing to talk about it in relation to bipolar disorder. If shared, his capabilities were then questioned, and he was looked at through another lens. Or at least he believed that. Many others did too. He didn't want to be treated differently. I understand that now, and I still thought something needed to change. He was human, and sometimes he legitimately needed to call in sick. So what? If he couldn't take care of himself, he couldn't go to work. And the careers he'd started, the jobs he'd lost, I'd lost count how many there were. This was a big deal. But selfishly, what did it have to do with me and a potential diagnosis?

Curious to find out, and knowing I couldn't have this conversation while waiting at a multi-floor apartment entrance with noise from the apartment above, I put Dad on hold to grab my winter jacket. I'd feel better outside anyway. I always do. I brushed past my boyfriend without saying a word. Only a couple of times with trusted friends had I gotten drunk thus far, or I'd gone overboard by myself or with a date. No expectations and no upset for anyone else except me the next day. My boyfriend was having a good time, and I thought, *I'll leave him there, he'll be fine, I'll be fine. I can handle this.* He probably wouldn't even notice or care. I hurried past them all and exited the building, happy to be outside at last, although not happy about the situation at hand.

"So what happened?" I asked as soon as the fresh winter air hit my face. I adjusted my black boot zipper slightly so that my jeans wouldn't get caught on them and stumbled over the snow-filled sidewalk. It was January, after all. In Chicago.

"Do you want to talk to Mom?"

"No, Dad, I want to talk to you."

He didn't answer my original question. I guess he didn't want to and wanted his wife to answer for him. It was another failure, another reason he couldn't support his family. Another job loss was not fun. I'd been there myself, and I understood. I didn't want Mom to have to explain or avoid my questions either. Besides, she didn't say I had bipolar disorder. Dad did. Nothing had been answered, and I thought Mom would justify the accusation of a diagnosis and/or ignore my question about what happened. I knew what happened. Dad obviously wasn't well. Also, I was scared. Maybe I was bipolar.

"Dad, are you okay?"

Silence for a second. Longer than usual. I waited, having flashbacks to the phone conversations when Dad was in the hospital. But this time Mom was with him. This time I was an adult. This time I wasn't as reactive as I was at seventeen. Maybe therapy was helping.

He then said something interesting that I thought someone who had bipolar disorder couldn't tell.

"I don't feel alright. I feel off."

Silence.

"Do you want to talk to Mom?" he asked again. I heard the shuffling of the phone because he didn't wait for me to answer this time. I understood more of the story from Mom.

"Dad's not doing well," Mom told me what actually happened. "He couldn't remember where he parked at work. He apparently was wandering around at school, unsure of where to go next."

I could hear the distress in Mom's voice, and the habitualness of it. I would guess that she wanted this to be the final manic episode. She had been through enough. So had he. "I had to go and pick him up. And, he needs a doctor's note to go back."

"So he didn't lose his job?" I inquired.

"Not yet," Mom said.

I imagined him wandering around his work, wondering where to go, and perhaps asking a trustworthy individual. Then being pulled into a room and being told to not come back. Not without a doctor's excuse. I couldn't imagine it clearly. Dad taught students with special needs at the fourth through sixth grade level. What would it be like to be in his shoes? What would it be like to not remember your schedule, knowing that you're doing something wrong and not being able to recognize it to save face? Especially because you've had the same schedule day after day. That would be so frustrating and humiliating.

Good thing Mom had been there. Good thing that she could go get him. Good thing that they're still together. I figured out part of the story. And the unanswered question remained: *Why did Dad say I could have bipolar disorder right now?*

I knew the timing was exactly right. I had just talked about it with my therapist last week. It's like I was preparing for this call. Thank you, Universe/God/Whatever you want to call it.

◆ ◆ ◆ ◆ ◆

In the therapist's office, I had waited to bring up my fear around this for over a year. Anything important would come up at the end of a therapy session. Therapists call that a "doorknob confession." I had been wondering ever since Lauren told me about Dad at sixteen. I finally had the guts to say it.

"I just have always been nervous that I might be bipolar," Long pause of fear inserted here, me realizing I needed to ask a question, get confirmation, and a response from her: "C... could I be?"

"To be honest," she answered, my heart started beating faster, knowing that we had only five minutes left of our session, knowing that this was the question that had plagued me since I realized the extent of my dad's illness. If anyone in the family would have it, it'd be me. I mean, look at me. The emotions. The upset. The inability to communicate effectively. The ups. The downs. *What if that explained it? It could be this, right?*

I wasn't sure if I could handle the answer. *What if she said, "Yes"? Would I cry? What if that fear came true? How would that affect my family? My future family? How would that limit me?* I'd be so mad at my parents and at God.

Would she respond in a way where I would need treatment? My brain went down the rabbit hole in the couple of seconds that I was waiting. I'd already been talking to her for over a year. *Would she have told me before? What if this was when I found out? I was left out of everything. What if this was the moment that my therapist told me her professional opinion was that I had bipolar disorder?* Bipolar disorder could be genetic, could skip a couple of generations, but I was too scared to look up the symptoms still. I was too scared to self-diagnose. *What if this was the time that she told me that I had it? How would I live with myself? How could I put anyone through what Dad had put me through?* Obviously, I was still putting the blame on my parents. I still didn't understand why they didn't tell me. And right now, I was only focused on one thing again: me.

My mind raced. Thoughts swirling. I sat, tense, on the chair I had rushed into that day. I hadn't wanted to be there. I was always late. She was used to it by now. I would rush in, plop down, and start talking about everything except the most important things. *What would she say?* Unsure. Nervous. *Could I even trust her?* I'd only seen her once a week; would she know what she was talking about? This was the first time that I had asked a question this serious. The long silence, she must be gathering her thoughts. Maybe she had to let go of the fact that I always waited until the end to bring up the thing I was most concerned about. Maybe I was just flustered, but it felt like a lifetime to hear her say, "I've seen trends of anxiety and depression, but not bipolar disorder."

Oh, my goodness. Sigh of relief. Immediately the tension released from my body, now relaxing. I'd brought this idea up only once before and tried to see how she responded to weigh if I should ask it directly. I was playing a game that the answer didn't matter to me. I *had* to look good. I didn't want to let anyone know that this question had kept me up at night ever since my dad went to the hospital that day.

Letting myself feel concerned and expressing that concern was huge. A breakthrough for me. I was finally expressing myself. Maybe I could have a mental illness. Maybe I wasn't 100% perfect. *Maybe there was something wrong with me.* Admitting I didn't know something and asking a professional was a big deal. I had asked for help, again.

I glanced up, waiting for the rest of her answer. What she said wasn't enough for me. I was trying not to look too interested because I had to pretend. I didn't want her to know that I was riding on this answer and wanted it in full.

She waited patiently until our eyes locked, and she leaned towards me and reassured.

"Jen, if you were bipolar, you would know already. There would have been extreme changes in your demeanor, and we would have determined that over a year ago when you first came into therapy. I see you suffering more from depression and anxiety than bipolar."

Having bipolar would have already shown up at this point.

I had to let that sink in. Be reassured. Again.

Besides my boyfriend, Madison was my only stability. I was starting to trust little by little, still separated from my parents in anger and frustration about how they didn't love me enough to tell me. In therapy, I was learning to express myself and the emotions that always haunted me.

I couldn't trust myself with my gut, either. Madison said that I had incredible emotional intelligence and intuition. I decided, long ago, I couldn't trust that. Picking and choosing who I could trust with what, I wanted someone else to see everything important for me. Just like with everything, I relied on other people to tell me what I was like. I relied on other people to direct me where I should go with my career. I relied on others to tell me the most important things. This time, it worked in my favor by giving me the confirmation I needed to move on from this underlying worry. Just in time.

◆ ◆ ◆ ◆ ◆

Back in the present after my visit with my therapist, I asked Mom to put Dad on the line.

I paused and took a deep breath as he repeated himself.

"Jenny, but you know you could be bipolar. You have the tendencies towards it and it is genetic…"

Confidently, I replied. "No, Dad, I'm not bipolar. I'm sorry you lost your job, but I'm not bipolar. I'm twenty-five years old, and there is no possible way. There would have been traces of it by now. I know that I am the most emotional out of our family, and with those extreme emotions that I show, I would have seen it by now. I'm not bipolar, Dad. I have anxiety and depression, but not bipolar."

Thank God, my therapist indirectly taught me how to say that. Thank God, she had been there to help me express my emotions for myself and to Dad now. Maybe he was surprised at what I said, or maybe he knew I was at a point that I wouldn't listen anymore, so after this, he dropped it and eventually handed Mom the phone.

Mom mentioned how Dad would be changing his meds, probably sometime soon. As she sighed, I asked her if she was okay. She said she was, and I knew that was that. I began to see what my Mom had to go through. This was the beginning of seeing Mom more as I did when I was younger, as the best Mom in the whole wide world. This time for different reasons. She loved me enough to bring it up that I could be bipolar another time that year, and I confidently replied without concern. I wasn't bipolar. I didn't have bipolar disorder. That wasn't me.

After calming down by talking to a friend on the phone, I numbly went back into the apartment. I saw the same people, my boyfriend across from me, making jokes and fitting in. There was no way that I could continue in this night. When I hung out with these people, I judged myself for leaving my teaching career. They reminded me of stability and consistency and the smarts that I had given up on to become what, a waitress? Even more terrible, I was judging my boyfriend when he didn't take care of me the way I expected. He had no idea the terrifying conversation I had just had. He didn't understand where I was coming from or what I was thinking. *I mean, shouldn't he know what triggers me? Shouldn't he know I had just been triggered?* I had this "prince in shining armor" complex that I expected my first real boyfriend to be. He was my first love. No one could be that "prince" I was looking for. Ever.

I had unrealistic expectations not just for him, but myself and his people. I separated myself from his buddies from work, and really everyone. I would get mad at him when he didn't know when I was upset and when he couldn't tell, I felt left out from an intelligent conversation. I see now that this cut me off from learning. I didn't see how trapped I was in expressing anything. At this time in my life, I believed I would never make enough money nor have the right job, would never travel the way I dreamed I would, nor have the man of my dreams—the one I wanted to be married to and have babies with. That could never happen. These triggers were in the way. The emotions. Up and down. In and out. Only showing up as tears. I was trying hard to express myself the "right way." Maybe I was trying too hard. Meanwhile, I was getting closer to why I was upset about things, but not truly understanding that people weren't like me. Grateful for the patience of my therapist and boyfriend, as those were the people I trusted most. I didn't realize I would jump from one emotion to the next without skipping a beat. Of course, my boyfriend couldn't keep up. I couldn't even keep up. So then, who could?

Could I figure out what I was feeling? One sentence was anger. One sentence was devastation. Another was frustration. I thought he was the one who talked in circles, and that's why our problems didn't feel resolved at the end of the conversation. The emotions bouncing around up and down, an emotional high of sorts. All coming from me.

I was the emotional high.

I couldn't regulate my emotions. I was "overwhelmed" and "tired" until I burst. I didn't see my own power. I didn't see how my emotion was my superpower, this ability to connect to other people at this level. I didn't give my boyfriend a chance. With patience though, he tried. He gave me the time and space to explore sexuality, emotions, and relationships together, as a team, in a way I'd never experienced before.

I see now that I would take everything personally. I would even take it into the present. I was (am) too emotional. There was (is) something wrong with me. It always was (is) my fault.

Or it was his fault, easily deflecting from me what I was avoiding. He had no choice except to be the brunt of it. And it wasn't just him, but my entire family, my whole community, they were always at the brunt of my critique, judgment, and upset at the injustices happening against me, against humanity. If you said something and I realized you were not on my side, that was it. You were gone. One second I was completely connected to your life and story, and the next, bye! *It's easier that way. For both of us. You'll never understand anyway. You'll never "get" my complexity.* I didn't, so how could you?

I felt that there would always be a "them" and I wouldn't ever be accepted or liked fully. "They" can't relate. "They'll" never see. "They'll" never understand. I didn't see this "they" versus "me" was isolating myself over and over by making a "they" exist. I only wish I had seen it sooner. I could have related to my boyfriend's friends. I could have learned something from them or enjoyed them more thoroughly. I guess hindsight truly makes things 20/20.

I wouldn't be surprised if my boyfriend and I fought that night. We usually did when I was emotional. Me expecting him to know something was wrong, expecting him to detect when I felt isolated. I had all of these unreasonable expectations for him and for myself.

"Are you okay?" he asked as we settled into bed.

"No." I wouldn't say anything else. I couldn't say anything else. Exhausted, I started crying, and he pulled me in. Snippets of what went wrong, came out for sure as I cried. *This isn't how it's supposed to look.* Confused. Discombobulated. Unclear. Processing. Exhausted.

Tears ran down my cheeks as my boyfriend cuddled me to sleep. He held me as I closed my eyes, wishing this day was over, wishing that everything would be okay, and knowing that it never will be the same. I had stuck up for myself in a way I'd never done before.

With confidence that I did not have bipolar disorder, I would never be the same again.

CHAPTER SEVEN

Thanks Mom, I Love You

"CAN YOU PLEASE TAKE THIS WITH YOU?" I asked Dad, showing him the huge blue bin taking up the entire back seat of my Mazda3 sedan.

He had already answered, but I wanted to make sure this stuff was there when he drove the van fifteen hours from Chicago to Boulder, Colorado. I had to ask twice. I had to be reassured that something would be done. I never trusted that someone heard me the first time or that they would remember to do things for me. My insecurity was now totally annoying as an adult.

"What's in there?" he asked, looking at me quizzically.

"It's all of my winter stuff and artwork. Can you make sure you give it to Uncle Mike or Carly?"

"Yeah, that's fine."

He was distracted. I could tell he wasn't listening. I could see his mind racing even though there was nothing to have it race about, in my eyes. He was trying to do everything so quickly. He seemed to be walking around in circles, not achieving anything. Mom had called me the previous day and told me what was up.

"Dad's definitely having an episode now, Jen. I don't know whether he should go to Colorado. He hasn't been sleeping, and I'm worried about him. I just don't know what to do."

I reassured Mom that everything would be okay. If he was that terrible, we'd just have to tell him he couldn't go.

"He won't listen to me. He's going," Mom knew that when he gets into this state, he has to see something's up for himself in order to make a change. Unfortunately, she couldn't do anything. Mom hadn't always shared this information. Maybe she thought I could make a difference with him. Maybe I thought I could too.

I had shown up with my own agenda to have Dad take my stuff, so I'd be set up for success for the winters in Colorado. I was finally moving there after three years of wanting to. Now that my stuff was taken care of, I was happy to help him, however I could. When I asked if he had packed, he walked away without responding, not present, scrambling, and I could barely hear, "Almost."

I knew that meant, "Nope, haven't started." So, I took over in the same way I usually do. I helped him pack, step by step. Bag in hand, we talked about what was necessary for the ten days that he was going to be in Colorado.

I was excited that he was willing to go and begin his travels in this capacity. I hadn't ever seen Dad take a trip by himself without Mom. *How liberating!* I thought as we discussed what clothes to bring, where he was planning to stay, and which family members he'd see. The conversation took place sporadically, as he would leave the room suddenly, again and again. I would wait for him to come back and continue. I personally was happy he was taking time off. This summer had to be hard for him. He'd been stressed out this past year, switching jobs again, and he commuted all the way to Chicago every day through that traffic. He deserved this.

Career and job changes were common for Dad. In my lifetime, he'd been a painter, a real estate agent, a teacher, and a teaching assistant. Before I was born, there were even more. I felt I hadn't seen him hit his stride in his career. Maybe this was the freeing experience he needed to find the exact thing that he loved! I felt travel did that for me, which is why I yearned for it so much.

Bipolar disorder was a great "excuse" to be fired. Or at least the inconsistencies that came with bipolar disorder were a great reason. Although legally, an employer couldn't fire someone for a diagnosis, it could definitely affect the way people interact with you. My dad could attest to that. With the secrecy of mental illness in our world, Dad told me he's still scared to mention anything about it to employers or potential employers. He never knew what to do as he applied for different jobs over the years. Does he write in that he has been hospitalized in an application or leave it blank, hoping they won't notice? Or, does he lie? Would they not invite him for the interview if they knew?

He would question and debate, not knowing the right answer because there wasn't one. Would it change the way people worked with him? How long would he last in that position if/when he had an episode? Applying for disability had been nearly impossible. Having been rejected a couple of times, it took calls upon calls, forms upon forms. When he finally got it, he still had to work through the stigma. Every time he applied for another job, what approach would he choose to take?

Being let go is not easy. I thought teaching was my thing, just like Mom and Dad. Mom had switched jobs to be a trader at a major investment company, and Dad had gone back to teaching. I knew what it was like for me to be fired—"asked to resign"—it's devastating.

After college graduation and applying to jobs all summer, I had two options I would have been happy with: becoming an outdoor instructor at an education center in Massachusetts or a teacher at one of the schools where I did my student teaching. The yearlong student teaching program I did at Illinois State University had brought me to Woodland Middle School (in between Lupe and the second semester's cooperating teacher) where I was a "bilingual push-in teacher." There, Mr. Lopez walked me around for a couple of months to every classroom that had one of our bilingual students in it. I observed, and occasionally, I co-taught with the teachers we visited each day. Having been exposed to each teacher's unique style, I knew who to go to for what. I knew who to ask for what, and I felt supported. My decision was made clear when I went in for an interview for an English teacher position, and they offered me the job on the spot. I had told myself, "I would teach if I got the job at Woodland." So I retracted my outdoor educator acceptance, found an apartment in the neighborhood just north of the school, and off I went, planning into the summer. I made my way to my first day as an official teacher.

With smaller class sizes and a supportive team, I could see my own potential for growth. I worked hard, using my unique abilities and fresh-out-of-college inspiration to create thematic lessons, incorporating rubrics, exploring themes, and having sixth and seventh graders write every day. It wasn't until thirty days after the start of school that I received a call from the office in front of my class.

"Miss Kraakevik, come see Mr. Garcia after this period. We're sending a substitute for your third-period class."

"Is everything okay, Miss K?" one of my students asked. The kids knew something was up. My face couldn't hide it.

"Yeah, yeah." I ignored the obvious lie I just told them and moved on to give the homework assignment, making the last couple minutes of class focused. You see, the next period was my prep period. I had no students. No substitute needed. I knew something was up, having to see the principal, but I knew him. I wasn't worried about that. It was the substitute that shifted the emotions that showed on my face.

I walked into his office to learn about thirty-day cuts in Chicago because of low enrollment. I was the last one hired, first one fired. And then he graciously drove me to the substitute teaching office in Chicago Public Schools because he knew I didn't have a car. In a flash, I had lost my job. I became a displaced teacher and could immediately place myself as a substitute in Chicago, but that wasn't my dream. That wasn't what I said yes to. I second guessed again. *Is teaching really my thing?*

Being let go based on nothing more than enrollment after seeing progress with inner-city kids, and canceling my other opportunity was devastating to me because it wasn't my choice.

Dad's circumstances were different, yet he also understood. Sometimes he would lose his job due to the illness and being sick. Dad has what's called rapid cycling bipolar disorder. Rapid cycling is not a separate diagnosis—it is a "specifier" to the diagnosis of bipolar disorder. It simply means that within a year, the person living with bipolar disorder has four or more mood episodes, whether that's ups or downs (mania or depression) or a combination of both. It means that the ups and downs occur more often and are more a part of his daily life. And that's what I saw in my dad.

It's not easy to keep a job, especially without the transparency and support Dad needs.

He thought it was dangerous to take a break that summer. When he's not busy, he is at risk for an episode. When he's too busy, he's at risk too. It's terrifying not to know when to trust yourself.

One of my uncles said it the best, "It must be a living hell for him." Not knowing when to make a move or not. Does he trust that his productivity is actually him, or is it the mania that's driving it? Another manic episode could lead to hospitalization if he didn't catch it early enough. Dad had his own way of dealing with his illness, and his career is one of the ways he was affected.

"Okay, Dad, you have enough packed, so then, do you have your meds ready?" I couldn't believe that question came out of my mouth. Just a few years ago, I would have never imagined having this conversation. I knew medication was a part of his life, but talking about them was another story. When I brought it up, Dad conceded. He started bringing me his meds. Capsule by capsule, bottle by bottle, I asked him how many of each one that I would put in his medicine organizer, reminding him that he didn't have to bring the whole bottles for only ten days. We talked back-and-forth as I halved what he needed half of and then made it so that he could pack it all away. Having clothes, toiletries, and now his meds packed, he was ready to go. This is where I became nervous. He was closer to getting in the car and driving away, like this.

He still wasn't present. He wasn't excited. He was stressed and unfocused. He was having an episode, just like Mom had said. I couldn't believe I saw it too.

We put his things in the van, and he ran back inside to grab one more thing. He didn't say anything about it to me, so I stood there confused. I couldn't figure out what to do. Mom had already tried to tell him not to go. I turned to him as he jumped into the driver's seat.

"Are you sure that you should go? I mean, you don't seem good right now, Dad."

He avoided eye contact and said, "Yes, it'll be fine. I've got to get this van to them. They need it right away. I'll be fine. I'll stop as soon as I am closer than here."

With fifteen hours ahead of him, traveling by himself, I knew I couldn't go with him. Mom couldn't go with him either. In the scope of all that was happening, I was concerned. And I couldn't do anything. Helpless. Worried. Uncertain.

"Be safe then, Dad. If you feel like you need to stop, just stop."

"Okay, okay." It seemed he had barely heard, his face looking backward as he turned the van into reverse. "Bye."

"Love you."

"Love you too."

I watched from my parent's house as he drove off. My eyes started to tear up, watching the van drive away. I knew I would never see the van again, but I just hoped I would see the man in the front seat, back safely and in one piece.

He did make it to his brother's house in Colorado. I learned years later that Dad had called Mom shortly after he drove away and decided to stay in a hotel room for the night. He recognized he wasn't doing well. I hope I contributed to that realization in some way. At the time, I was hoping and praying that Dad would be okay as it happened. When he arrived, his brother and niece and nephews didn't see the mania, the weirdness, or the extra stuff that Dad brought with him on that trip. I learned that he had gone for long walks and didn't tell anyone where he was going. But I wasn't there for that. I wasn't monitoring, analyzing, or judging him. But I was worried.

I was concerned that he would have an episode and not be close to the doctor who could help him if he needed to be hospitalized. I wondered if Mom would have to spend an exorbitant amount of money to go jump on a last-minute flight, save the day, and make sure he was okay. I was afraid he couldn't make the drive by himself. *What if someone wouldn't know to help him? What if he couldn't help himself?*

Fear. Worry. Anxiety.

Never had I ever thought traveling could be a bad idea. After teaching and waitressing, I had become a flight attendant because I thought it would be fun to travel the way I'd always wanted to. In hindsight, traveling then maybe wasn't right for Dad. With both of us as adults, I could only help as much as I could. He had to help himself too.

How do you determine that line of when to leave him be? How do you determine when he's not okay to help himself? Seeing this perspective, I had no idea how Mom did it. I had no idea how she could stay and live with it, every single day. My uncles (Dad's brothers) all said that my mom was a saint, an angel, a good Christian woman, and wife.

And I knew it. I hadn't told her how amazing she was. I didn't know how to express it to her, nor did I realize the extent of what she actually had done for us. It wasn't until a year later when I was twenty-eight that I called and told her.

"Mom, I just wanted to thank you."

"For what, Jenny?"

My eyes started tearing up. She had no idea what was coming. This was out of the blue. This was something I meant to tell her before, but I didn't know how.

"Mom," my voice cracked. "You have been there for Dad and for all of us more than you know. Your generosity. You've made it possible for us to be as amazing as we are. Even as you were handling everything with Dad, his…" I paused. Tears streamed down my face in recognition of what I was saying. I adore Mom. I adore her, and I hadn't said it enough. "Bipolar disorder. You did it all by yourself. I want you to know that you're not alone anymore. We kids are all adults now and we love you. I love you."

"I love you too, Jenny." I could hear her voice waver. I knew she had heard me.

I would not be the same person without her. She did her best. She loves me, and I love her. It had come full circle with Mom, and I was so happy that God gave me such a caring role model in my life.

That conversation, I will always remember. Emotional. Expressive. Powerful. As beautiful as I learned Mom was/is, I was beginning to see that I could be beautiful too. Within the tears and emotions. That perhaps I have access to my feelings more than others do. Maybe there isn't anything wrong with me. Maybe, just maybe, I was gaining the strength to let my vulnerabilities actually be me. Perhaps my vulnerability, my sharing myself, my ability to stick up for myself and be with my mom and dad with whatever they had to say, that was the strength I had been looking for. I took back my power with my parents. And I did it with love. Exactly how I wanted it to be. Freedom. Love. Grace. I finally gave myself the opportunity to truly appreciate Mom for who she is. That moment will never go away, just like the moment Dad and I had when I was at that party years ago. These moments are stuck with me forever. Ingrained in my soul. Forged in my breath. Etched in my heart.

SECTION II: HOW TO OPEN UP THE CONVERSATION WITH YOUR FAMILY

Introduction to
Section Two

I WAS TWENTY-SIX AND CALLED DAD WHEN I REALIZED
I needed to share something.

"Dad?"

"Hey Jen, what's up?"

"I've been pretending that everything's okay, and it's really not."

My heart was pounding, my mind racing. I continued.

"I spent this whole time judging you for the way that you told me
about your bipolar disorder," imagine tears starting here, voice
breaking, the whole gamut, "when I never really asked you what it's
like."

"Yeah... it hasn't been easy."

"I can only imagine. And Dad, all I really want is a loving and
connected relationship with you."

He wanted that too. He had been there with me and for me every
step along the way. The separation I had created from him as a
teenager was only mine because of my judgment of what I thought
they should have done, for not telling their kids about bipolar
disorder. I doubt any parent expects to have that conversation when
they imagine what parenthood looks like. That same day, I declared
in a room full of people that I would make a difference around the
conversation about mental illness. How that was going to show up,

I had no idea. Dad and I had the above conversation in July. Almost six months later, December 2016, I decided I needed to actually do something about it.

I recall calling Alex, one of my friends who told me to write this story. Now at twenty-eight, I was freaking out and trying to talk myself out of approaching Dad about his illness again. She reassured me. "You've got to do this. It's important, not just for you, but for the people you want to help with your book."

Who said I was going to write a book? All I was talking about was speaking with Dad that day, although secretly, that was my dream. I had let it slip that I wanted that. As a good friend, she pushed me towards it.

So I decided on the phone that I was going to talk to him about his medications. It was a way to bridge the conversation, like I had a year ago when I helped him pack for Colorado.

I started the conversation in the context of: What if we started talking about his illness more? How could we do it? Would Dad be willing? I shared with him how I wanted to make a difference in mental illness in the world. I'm sure it was awkward and uncertain. It definitely was more unplanned than I felt comfortable with. More importantly, I shared that I didn't know how to do it. When I asked him if he would be willing to talk about it, he said yes.

We brainstormed about how we could do that with the distance, him in Chicago and me in Denver. We then came up with the idea of writing on Google Drive together. Dad and I have always enjoyed writing; he used to help me with my papers in high school. We would read what I had come up with aloud and edit it together. I loved those times together, and it turned out Dad did too.

That next week, Dad started our Google document. I couldn't believe it. We decided to call our writing "Letters to my Daughter," to connect, explore, and talk about "his illness," as Mom calls it. This platform opened up more conversations. It developed into us thinking we would compile our writing together. Eventually, we could make a book out of it. I was driven with the outline and organization (I know—finally I'd learned it!), hoping we could put our experiences side-by-side. I thought we could organize it by emotion, including mania, depression, and whatever my emotions were so that readers could connect to our story. After a year of writing, from January 2017 to April 2018, we set up a time to discuss it. Awkwardly, of course. There, I realized three things:

1. I had more words organized around creating a book about bipolar disorder.

2. There were fewer resources out there from a daughter's perspective.

3. I was waiting for Dad to say yes to what I wanted for the book.

That last one was huge, as I determined that I needed to do this for me. I couldn't wait for approval from Dad anymore. I was an adult. I realized I could decide what I wanted this book to look like. I also recognized how this could make a big difference and determined I had to go for it.

It came up often that I needed to do this for you, my reader. Every time I brought up what I was working on for my book with my coworkers (I work with new people every shift), every single person had something to say about mental illness. Either they experienced it themselves, or their family member or friend had it. All of those conversations catalyzed me towards this book completion. Their stories pushed me not to let it go.

Dad was now telling me things we had never spoken about in real life. He was so open, available, and free to talk about it in our writings. It was shocking, especially since we had kept this private, only the occasional mention or sporadic conversation, as seen in my story above. Now, the floodgates were open.

When I asked Dad if I could talk to his brothers, he said yes too. I thought maybe that would stop the project. I was kind of hoping for it. All of these conversations were *terrifying*. I'd never done anything like this before.

Dad and I planned to have those conversations together with one uncle at a time. Instead, it ended up being phone calls between each uncle and me. Dad said, "It's probably for the better. They may share more without me on the line." Maybe. I guess we'll never know.

I had asked them each for the conversation via email, saying that Dad was okay with it, and that I wanted to record the conversations upon their approval.

I also told them the current goals of the book:

1. Let people understand that they are not alone if they have a family member diagnosed with bipolar disorder (or a mental illness).

2. To convey that nothing is wrong with a mental illness.

I couldn't believe it when all my uncles said yes.

It took a couple of weeks to complete all of the uncle interviews in September and the beginning of October 2018. I had written a list of questions to ask them, which you'll see in Chapter 11. Within that list and the interview itself, I decided to give myself the freedom to go with the flow of the conversation. My uncles and I do not always have one-on-one conversations on the phone, so this was fun and challenging in itself. We were talking about something that we've never talked about *ever*. It was monumental in our family. My cousin told me afterward that she was called by each one of my uncles (obviously, one of them was her own father), asking what to do with what Jenny wanted to talk about.

"Be honest," she told them, "That's all she wants."

To say the least, she was right. My uncles were uncomfortable with this conversation too? How have we not talked about it before? *They brought it up to my cousin first? Woah. I should stop there. I shouldn't continue, right?*

Thank goodness I had already set up the conversation via email and told them what I wanted to talk about. If left to my own devices, I would have chickened out. I naturally didn't want to say, "What was it like for you to have a brother diagnosed with bipolar disorder?" It seemed awkward, weird, and *why am I doing this again?* It was so much easier to write about it. Heart pumping, nervous about which direction this conversation would go, I worried as soon as I said hello on the phone. *What would they say? Were they just being nice by offering to talk to me about this? What do they actually know about bipolar disorder? And, what was Dad really like when he was first diagnosed?* For a couple of those interviews, they had to bring it up, so I would start talking about bipolar disorder. They would say something like, "I know you wanted to talk about this..." *And why wasn't I again? Oh yeah, fear.*

I couldn't believe they helped me when this was something we both were uncomfortable talking about. They supported and loved me even when I didn't ask for it.

It took transcribing the conversations to see those trends. I had decided to transcribe them myself, to save money and to experience the calls again. I would write exactly what was said in the interviews on paper. Easy enough. As soon as reality set in, I avoided transcribing for months. I was scared of what I would discover, how the interviews actually went, and, to be honest, of the project itself.

I was afraid that it was all a waste of time, nothing was achieved, and it was all worthless. *Why did I say I would do this? Why are my coworkers asking me about it like I'm going to complete it? Why did I set myself up for this?*

Scared, upset, and frustrated, I pushed through. As I went through the interviews again, I watched myself and discovered how I responded to people when I was not comfortable. I noticed who I was, when I became upset and when I didn't. I found out I wasn't afraid to meet the person where they were and let the conversation go wherever it did. I also steered it back if we became off topic. I saw how much I genuinely care and how I listen to people.

As if those interviews weren't enough, I then asked to interview Mom, Lauren, Dan, and finally, Dad. *Why am I continuing to do this?*

I was convinced that my family members would ask me to stop. *This is too personal, Jenny—you can't do this—we will hate you if you do.* In one conversation with Mom, she brought up something I had asked Dad via text that day, asked me to be patient with him, and tried her best to answer the question. Then, she paused. *This is it. This is the final straw. I'll have to listen to Mom when she tells me I have to put this down now and give up.*

She surprised me by saying, "I'm so sad that we didn't tell you because of how much it hurt you. And there's nothing we can do about that now. We have to let it go."

Every conversation I had, I was waiting for someone to forbid that I write this.

Maybe then, I wouldn't have to do this. At this point, I felt compelled to continue regardless of my own personal feelings. I wanted to be able to blame it on someone else. My family didn't do what I expected. So, I had the opportunity to learn about everyone's memories and experiences. Through it, I realized something extraordinary.

No one knew what to do.

None of my family members had dealt with mental illness before, as far as I knew. They had to figure it out. Just like I have had to figure out what to do. I had to explore questions like:

Do I have it too?

Why don't we talk about this?

Why does this make us all so uncomfortable?

There's no formula. No right answer. Even the way I wished it had been done wasn't necessarily "right." A revelation. An epiphany! *So now what?*

Before going through this process, I was so busy making my parents wrong. As much as I understood conceptually that parenthood can be hard, I hadn't ever thought that they didn't know what to do. They weren't all-knowing like I had pictured them as a kid. They had to figure it out. Just like me.

It was through discovering what I needed to let go of, exploring my emotions, and taking on fear that this book could be written. I'm grateful my family and I continued to be willing to take it on.

Every time I interviewed and transcribed, I noticed something new and wonderful or completely debilitating and upsetting. I heard the wonderful things that my uncles said about both of my parents. I heard how my sister was struggling and how my brother reacted to circumstances now.

Mom didn't want to talk about it much, "It's too hard," she said herself in our interview, and we all knew it. Of course, it was hard, and she talked about it with me anyway. When I asked her what it was like when she couldn't say anything about Dad's illness, she said one word that changed my life.

"Strangling."

No one understood. She couldn't even check to see if someone else understood, because it had to be private. It wasn't acceptable to talk about. After hearing that, thinking about the times in the 90s and early 2000s (when I was in the picture), my love abounded for Momma even more.

Each family member had our part to play in this inquiry about Dad's bipolar disorder. When Mom didn't know what to do, she'd call over the uncle closest to where they lived. The one who could sit with Dad, have him over to his house, or be with him when she couldn't anymore. It dawned on me that it was hard for Dad. He was trapped in something that he knew impacted his family, and he couldn't do anything about it. Should he stay and cause trouble to his wife and young kids or run off and go away to prevent more harm? Should he talk about it and discover how they really feel? How could he, knowing how hard it is for himself to even speak about?

This section, *How to Open Up a Conversation with Your Family,* is a guideline, an explanation of what I did, and an option for you. You can use it as you explore how you want to have this conversation with your family. It also may not always work, and it definitely is not easy to do. I can only bring my experience and hope it can support you in how you want to talk about this with your people. Maybe my perspective will make it possible for you to talk about bipolar disorder in general. If you're anything like Dad and me, you might need someone else or another medium (writing) to facilitate. I discovered through completing this manuscript that Dad and I approach talking about bipolar disorder completely differently. My question for myself remained: *Am I willing to keep talking about it?*

For you, like me, it could take a couple of tries. Or many. You could avoid it and wonder if you'll ever be able to talk about your family member's mental illness. No worries. This is about practicing expressing yourself. You can decide how that looks for you, along with your focus and goal.

- Is it to open up about it?

- Is it to explore your own feelings?

- Is it to reduce stigma?

- Is it to find what you need for you?

You are the one to decide. That's what I want to guide you through here. My goals may not be the same as yours. Don't worry. You do you.

I want to express something about mental illness: we can't fix it for our family members or even for us. The more we sit with that, the more we let that be the truth in our lives, the more freedom we will have. Besides that, I still believe that there's nothing wrong with a mental illness. I have to keep writing it: there is nothing wrong with Dad.

Maybe this will work and you will find something that will support you and your family in this book. You could call that a solution. And, I'm not promising solutions here. Rather, I'm providing an experience of communicating with your family, not giving up, and having the tough conversations even when you're scared. That's what I'm interested in.

Communication is key. Being able to express yourself and be knowledgeable about this illness is necessary. This isn't something that will go away. There is no cure. It takes time to find what works for you and your family members. Do not give up. The searching process, the discovery process that I talk about in My Story is something you can't step over. It's a necessary part of it.

If you are looking for your communication to be all neat and pretty, that's not what this is. Most of my conversations were awkward and weird to me. This process is unique, and it takes time. Communication about bipolar disorder is one of those lifelong discoveries that your family member will have to fight for every day for the rest of their lives. And you, as their family member, will have to, too. If you so choose. Realizing that about my dad was debilitating, and I kept naturally wanting to fix it all. I wanted to make it go away for my mom, my sister, and my brother. I wanted to make the trends of mental illness *stop* in my own family.

But that isn't treating it like it is a natural part of life. Mental illness diagnosis happens to people and we all have our own ups and downs. Maybe you've felt depressed like I have. Or maybe you are also living with a mental illness. Maybe you're looking for the answer for yourself, to try to fix you. Because there must be something wrong with you. That has to be it. Like what I thought about myself and my emotions. In a sense, the impact of bipolar disorder became the way that I encountered my own experiences. It's only one piece in a more cohesive puzzle, even when it feels all consuming. I can't stress enough that there isn't anything wrong with the emotions or overwhelm. It's okay.

This is the time to *not* be afraid to explore mental illness. Or you can be afraid, like me, and act anyway. Sometimes there's an opening right in front of our eyes. Other times, it's about creating the opening. I created a conversation with my family, and I want to share it with you, the ins and outs and ups and downs, and how I explored it. I recommend that you express yourself in the way that will be most freeing to you. You decide that too. Take my advice for what it is, not perfect, not the answer, and definitely not the solution. It is just my way.

Allow yourself to play and make mistakes here. Allow yourself to recognize what is going on in yourself. Develop your emotional intelligence and start using the tools that you learn. See whether they work for you and your family. Sometimes they will, and sometimes they won't. We have to endure through the trial and error. We have to learn how to communicate about our own feelings. We have to give grace to our family members who might not live up to what we expected of them.

So here's what I did, and I hope it helps you. This is to discover what it is that gives you the most freedom and joy around bipolar disorder in your life. Remember, the whole time you explore this that you're not alone.

You're not the only one.

I hope this provides you a chance to support yourself and the means to move forward in your life like I have. I hope that you start conversations that you've never had, and that you start saying something new about this.

It's time. The time is now.

CHAPTER EIGHT

Dad Asks How He Can Help

I HAD BEEN TALKING ABOUT BIPOLAR DISORDER directly (in writing) with Dad for over two years. I had already interviewed all of our family members; Dad was the last one. And, yet, here I was, struggling with talking about it with the person who, at one point, was going to write this book with me.

Dad once told me I needed to pick my battles. I understand why he said that now. Trying to emotionally express every unmet expectation is exhausting. Especially with all of the emotions I have. What he didn't realize is that I needed to express all of this so I could move on. The whole process was scary, especially because I wasn't sure what the people I love and trust would say on the other line. I wanted to express what bipolar disorder meant to me. Talking to my family members was frustrating, slightly ridiculous, and completely terrifying. It still is.

My conversation with Dad was set up the same as the other interviews. The emotion was stronger because, in my eyes, there was a lot more at stake. There was still a part of me that didn't want to upset him. This conversation was bound to have us both upset.

The question that lingered in our writing, and in this conversation, was, "What to do next?" That was the title for our new Google Drive document. I was proud of us. We had written close to 600 pages together. Those pages consisted of the normal "how are yous" and "how was your day's" of a father-daughter relationship, and also questions and answers about bipolar disorder. I'd never felt closer to my dad.

At thirty years old, I finally said exactly what I discovered I wanted from this whole thing.

"Are you available now, Dad?"

"Yeah, sure, let me just get into the house, and I can call you back. Or, can you call me back in a couple of minutes, and I'll then be inside."

Perfect. Yet my heart was racing. I didn't know what to do. I brought it up so nonchalantly, like it was no big deal, when it was. My heart pumped out of my chest. *Why did I ask? I'm not ready for this. I should have waited.* I knew that I could keep saying that for days, months, or even years.

"I could just wait..." would curse me and keep me in the same conversation, nothing. Fear. *What if it didn't go well? What did I make myself do? Why am I so nervous?*

I called him back on a recorded line and asked him if it's okay to record it, as per my family interview protocol. He made a snide comment, asking if it could be used in the court of law. I joke back, laughing, connecting, and avoiding.

"I don't know how to talk about this..." I finally said.

He responded, "Just talk."

What do you know; Dad gave me room to open up. Just like my uncles and other family members did. And my theory about "who Dad is" debunked once again. You see, I have a perspective that Dad is someone who waits to have someone bring up bipolar disorder. And that I'm the one who has to start the conversation. Here, Dad is starting it. *Where did I come up with that "true" perspective?*

We talked about how different it was talking versus writing, and how I wanted to be able to bring it up in person versus just writing. He responded and asked,

"How can I best help at this point? Or, is just communicating how you feel helpful for you? I think by now you probably understand all of the components."

Dad recognized a couple of things here:

1. I needed help, not just with bringing it up, but also with how to process this.

2. He validated my emotions and my need to say how I feel.

3. I'm smart enough to understand all of the actual physical/practical pieces about bipolar disorder.

Here was the thing for me: It wasn't the understanding piece that made the difference. I had learned a lot about bipolar disorder (after avoiding it for years), read books, taken the National Alliance on Mental Illness (NAMI) Family to Family class, talked to people, etc. Through all of that, it still didn't feel like enough. How do you "know enough" about an emotional mood disorder when everything is attached to unpredictable emotions? It's unsettling and will always be unsettling. We can't know it all regarding bipolar disorder. Even knowing about it doesn't always apply to *us*.

How do I respond? What do I say?

I interrupted awkwardly, apologized, and asked him to continue, deciding not to listen to my thoughts. I understand the components. I understand what is going on, and I hadn't really said it clearly. Dad continued. Thank goodness.

"But, maybe that doesn't necessarily help resolve it."

Wait a second. *Resolve?* We think there's a way to resolve this? Maybe I needed to communicate something. *Come on, brain, what do I actually want to say? I wanted something different, maybe?* So many people have this. It isn't who Dad is. It's just another part of life that Dad has the opportunity to show me.

How could he really help? What was this really about? Why am I being so weird about this? We've talked about this. We've done this. What is wrong with me? Back up. Rewind. Stop talking, Jen. Abort mission. Then I opened my mouth.

"I guess, you know, Dad, it's never going away." *Oh no, what have I done, he's going to be responding shortly—did I say something wrong? How can I back out?* I keep talking, "I think that's the hard part. That's hard to grasp. Not that there's anything wrong with having ups and downs like mania and depression... it's just hard to grasp that it can't be fixed. There's no cure. There's no 'let's do this thing, and it's all better.' And, you never know how it's going to affect you, like if things are gonna happen that are from your illness or not, whether that's you or if it's not, and then as you grow and develop..."

I teeter off script. None of the questions I had were here. In fact, I didn't have a question list for this conversation. I'd already asked them in our writing. This was talking. *Can we talk about it?* Wander. Explore.

I expressed the concerns I had. Will things change for him on a dime? Will he experience something we can't support him with as a family? Who is Dad really?

I discovered right then that this was the point of the whole book, of the conversations. Of everything. I wanted to know my dad. In the complexity of all of the reasons why I came up with writing this book, I now see that I just wanted to get to know him. *What was his life really like, and how has a diagnosis changed it?* I wanted to get closer. This was my way to connect, love, and care about him and his experience of life. What I wanted from expressing myself was that I would have my dad in my life again. I felt I couldn't trust him because of the bipolar diagnosis secret. I yearned/ ached for this intimate, connected relationship with my dad. *What were his dreams and visions when he was young, and how have they changed now?*

Dad understood and told me how much more settled that it was for him. He'd had more of his life to process it. I had my teenage, naïve brain, and fifteen years hadn't been enough so far to break through the stigma and just have a conversation with my dad about this.

"I guess the real question for me is more how it affected you in the past, that's still probably something to resolve and how that affected you and affects you currently. How will it affect you in the future?" Dad asked.

"Now it affects me because I want to be open about this illness with our own family. I don't want the hesitancy that I've seen of our family members. I really feel this fear because I think people are going to shut down and not talk about it and step over it." I said.

"Every one of you has been exposed in one way or another to what's going on with me. And we know there isn't really, at least right now, some sort of resolution to the problem. It's not like I can take a magic pill or something." Dad pointed to what I had thought about the perplexity of this debate. There is no solution. The thing I don't think he considered was that maybe there was no problem. Maybe he's normal. Maybe there's nothing to fix. We kept talking.

I told him how weird it was for me to discover I can feel multiple emotions all at the same time. I was discovering what I'm capable of and also what was holding me back. I saw that sharing with family was important, but I thought I couldn't trust our family. I expressed my worry about the genetic component of bipolar disorder, all in the random, awkward way that I do it. I wanted the freedom to express myself, even if it wasn't perfect.

"I felt like I couldn't talk about certain things." I fumbled and asked him how I can support him.

"How do you support me?" he replied, making sure he understood. "Well, I don't really have that type of expectation. And I'm not really sure that I should. And, I'm not sure that you should have that expectation of yourself or of those other people around me. Other people have problems too—they just happen to be different than this."

I shouldn't have that expectation? I shouldn't expect myself to support him? Is that what Dad's saying? There must be something that I can provide for him or something that I can do to understand this. It will click, right? Isn't that how it works? Isn't that how I have discovered things in the past? Won't it work here?

He continued, "So there are all kinds of different ways, and you've kind of zeroed in on this, which is somewhat intriguing to me in one sense, because when we first started out, I thought it was, "Yeah, okay, Jen wants to know more about this. She wants to write about it and put together a book and so forth... yeah, I kind of get it." But, as we've written more and more and more, I thought to myself, okay this seems to go deeper than that. Why, I mean, I love writing to Jen. Sometimes it's painful, and it's good to think about it, yada yada yada yada. But why is this something that Jen keeps on pursuing so hard and so deep? And, I'm not sure I have the answer to that. And I'm not sure that... maybe there's not really an answer."

Defensiveness came up. *Why is she pursuing so hard and deep? Does he even realize how much this can affect someone? Does he see how much this affects Mom, Dan, and Lauren? Does he know? How doesn't he know?*

He kept talking. "Maybe it's all... what it seems to be. I mean, maybe I don't need to be reading anything into it. You've just got a project you want to work on, which is fine with me. But, getting back to the support. You've always supported and wanted to encourage me... and I've appreciated that a lot. And that's probably why we're close, and we're able to have these types of conversations. My condition didn't seem to affect the other kids as much as it's affected you. I don't know why that is. I don't think they felt necessarily betrayed or that it's affected their ability to relate to men. Everybody's different, but I'm not sure why that necessarily is true with you. I don't know why. It could be that it doesn't as much as you think, or that it affects your relationship with men. Maybe this partially is responsible or isn't all responsible or... I don't know the things that go into that mix."

I had to share how it's affected the family. "It could be that there were more effects than what you realize too, because we just happen to have this ongoing conversation about this."

He continued. "I had no idea it affected you as much as it has. Until I wrote the word betrayed, and you kind of hopped on that right away."

I rambled in response about how a recent ex had "betrayed me." Tears came down as I relayed my suffering about that circumstance, relating it back to the illness affecting the family and then how I wasn't told about it. After I calmed down in my rambling, it was his turn to react.

"What did you want me to say, that I'm bipolar?" He defended himself, his voice raised slightly in the way that Dad did it. I knew I had hit a button.

"Yeah," I said calmly.

"I mean, would you have really had a grasp of what that meant?" Still heated in the heightened awareness way it was, he was questioning what I had wanted and if I knew what that looked like in real life.

"No, but I didn't when I was told." I continued, "But the difference, I guess, what could have been... I would have liked to be able to have some of these conversations when I first learned about it. You know, when I was seventeen, and to say, "Hey Dad, I don't really get what this is... is that how it goes?" Or "Where should I look to find out more about this illness that's not a massive book? I wanted the support. I wanted to be able to discover it with someone who was an expert. You know this. I didn't at the time and still don't."

"You knew what was happening." Dad justified it.

"But I didn't though. Like, you think that a five-year-old brain can understand what's happening? You know what I mean? And then you add five more years, a ten-year-old brain, how would that one think? And I'm not saying that I didn't know that there was something up—I did. But I didn't know what it was."

I had finally said what I wanted to say. I wished that he had told me so I could have decided what to do with it myself. So I could have asked questions and been set up to talk about a difficult topic. Not just about bipolar disorder, but that practice could have helped me with other difficult topics. I would have liked to have the people I trusted in my life explain it to me. Or show me the resources they relied on. Dad and I responded defensively. We both knew it, and we both caught it. This means I didn't react nearly as badly as I could have. And it continued.

"Realistically, how would I have explained that to a ten-year-old kid?" He spoke louder and more directly. His defensiveness is obvious to me.

I responded quietly, "I don't know. That's exactly what I said. I don't know."

Then, Dad surprised me again. He said, "Maybe I could have handled it differently."

I didn't realize it, but I had wanted him to say that for years. He recognized my perspective. Inside, I sighed a breath of relief. I became relaxed, shoulders back, and my thoughts stopped swirling. What I had been fighting for had been achieved. He understood. Without a breath, he continued.

"At the time, that seemed to be the most expedient, the best way to handle things. Simply because I was very concerned that you or Dan or somebody else would say, 'Oh yeah, my dad's bipolar.' You know that's not a good thing. I'm not sure that you would have understood that this really could be a career limiting type of thing where it really could affect the family even more than it affects the family now."

He justified why he couldn't tell me at six, ten, or fifteen. I was a blabbermouth when I was comfortable, and yet still shy. You never know what a kid would do with this kind of information. It's perfect ammo that ignorance doesn't help with. Not knowing the repercussions of sharing my dad had bipolar disorder, not knowing what that even meant or how it showed up in my life. All of those were good reasons not to share about this with your kids. I could probably come up with a list of at least ten more reasons as to why not to tell me either. Including what I said, agreeing with him, in that next sentence.

"No, I know. I couldn't have understood that either. You're right." We talked about it. With Dad giving me my perspective, I realized that I could give him his own. He could be right too. I could finally see that he had his reasons and was simply doing the best he could.

"I couldn't afford to take that risk. I couldn't afford to take that risk." He repeated himself, maybe reassuring himself that he did the right thing. Or maybe that was what he said when he knew he was hurting one of his family members. "I can't take the risk" as a thought process totally makes sense because of the stigma, possible job discrimination, and community discrimination.

"No, you couldn't," I said. He truly couldn't. I finally understood. He couldn't say anything about this. He could have been paralyzed by fear, just like I had been. It could have been the fear of looking bad, that people would judge him, or that he wouldn't get another job if he lost it from exposing this. Or maybe it would get around, and then we kids would be discriminated against as well. The neighbors would potentially stop talking to us, or their parents wouldn't let their kids come over to our house if they knew. There was such a risk. I became aware of how much I hadn't thought about that perspective before. I was judging how he did it, again. And yet, we had *finally* talked about it. I understood. This conversation had me see it clearly. It took us long enough.

For a while, I believed he was more concerned with his image than what we understood as kids. I thought he was more concerned with the interpretation from the community. And that's who I thought Dad was. That's what I decided was true about him. That's what I had to come to understand about the reality of his life and my own. I had a father who was more concerned with his image than me. Ouch. Of course, I felt hurt.

In that moment of understanding and agreement, it hit me like a light bulb. It was the "click" I was waiting for, the same clarity I had heard in the conversation with my uncle.

Exactly like how the family didn't know what to do with him, he didn't know what to do with us.

He didn't know what was happening to him. Maybe he didn't know what to say to people. Maybe he didn't know how to express himself. Maybe he didn't know how to cover up his own emotions. As a man in our society, I'm sure he was taught that he couldn't be emotional with an emotional disorder. An impossible task! So, what if Dad didn't know what to do?

He did the only thing that he felt safe doing. He protected his daughter and his family. Turned out, it backfired. I wanted a relationship where I could be vulnerable with my dad about stuff that was important to me and our family, without stepping over it. I wanted to be close to him. When he cut me out of this part of his life, I felt disconnected. I felt uncertain. I felt confused. I wanted something different.

How could a Dad who loves me not tell me something? How could he do that to me? How could he do that to Mom? How could he not tell his family, his brothers, and anyone else? Why did he isolate himself? How could this be so secretive? How could he think that I would already know?

I wanted the "right" answer to come from my family. I wanted my questions to be answered by the people I trusted most. This time, they weren't, at least not at first. My parents had a chance to be vulnerable with me and show me how to be vulnerable in our family. They didn't take it when I wanted them to. I can't fault them for that. Having no safety at church, being afraid, and having little support: perhaps all of this took over. I'm sure they felt isolated, like they had to hide everywhere, alone and even scared. Just like we all feel sometimes. By talking to my dad, I began to realize that he was no less broken than me, and that together, we could piece back our relationship, one conversation at a time.

What do you do when you lose your best friend? Someone you wanted to be close with, but who never let you? Someone who you yearned to live with and who was there every second, but you were miles apart? That was me and my dad. I wanted to trust him, get his input, share our lives together, and write together. And it took the idea of this book to break the barriers. It took talking about it with him and gaining trust slowly but surely to get what I wanted. I reconnected with my dad. I could see him now as my friend, and a person I could trust, someone who will take time on the phone just because he loves me. Someone who can contribute to what I'm doing with his expertise and isn't afraid to tell me things without me becoming offended.

I discovered I wanted to connect with him again. I didn't want any topic to be off-limits. I didn't want there to be anything stopping me from having these conversations with him, or with anyone else for that matter. I didn't want the unanswered questions to keep mulling around in my head because expressing them to the person that it matters the most was terrifying. Turns out, I could be with him however he is. I could understand snippets of what he went through. And Dad loved me on the other side. When I became upset or when I brought up something that is hard to talk about, he still loves me. He still cares about me. He still wants me to have the best life I can.

The end of the conversation shifted to my mental illnesses, anxiety, and depression. By saying what we needed to say and letting go of the past, we talked about something that we had never talked about before. We learned anew who we both were as adults, and I could see how great we were with each other. We were vulnerable and shared what we were actually thinking. We were there for each other, asking clarifying questions and actually listening to one another, agreeing to disagree, and getting to the bottom of what we can do to help me let this go.

I expressed myself in spite of what I had to say being "disrespectful," "threatening," or "imperfect" in my eyes. And, I shared my discoveries with someone I'd been waiting to share with for a long time. I'd been waiting to share this with him, not realizing I had the power and capability to do it the whole time. I waited for the answers to these questions before I even knew the questions to ask. I'd been the one holding me back. It never was Dad.

I learned what was proper through my dad, I learned what was appropriate and professional and right, and now it's reflected back at me. All of the times that I thought he didn't have my back, was getting upset at me for no reason, all of the upset, the tears, the "crazy" I witnessed, that was all for me. I have a dad who loves me. He wants to be a part of my life every step of the way. My whole family does. They want to be there for me and care about me. They bring up stuff that is hard even when I think it's an attack on me. They're annoying and gracious and kind and loving. They're fearless, and they give me purpose in my life.

Who knew that, what I was looking for was exactly what I've already got?

◆ ◆ ◆ ◆ ◆

Thank you for reading up until this part. What happens now is a shift. You know I have shared my story up until this point, and this next part is entirely different, answering the questions "How does this apply to me" and "What is next for me?" It is a teaching section where I incorporate questions and ideas for conversations. I come with love, sharing my experience with you. Give me grace if it ever comes off as anything different than that. Enjoy.

CHAPTER NINE

What's In It for You?

HOW YOU INTERACT WITH YOUR FAMILY MEMBER diagnosed with bipolar disorder is not a science. There's no "right" way. There's only *your* way, *your* story, and *your* dream of what you want to happen with *your* people. For me, I gained more than I dreamed.

By being aware of how I respond and what I have to say by making myself to interact with it, I discovered how I think, what choked me up, and made connections that I would never have made by myself. I found out through talking with my family members that there were stories I had never heard. I learned who people were in my life at a deeper level and had the guts to ask questions I had never asked before.

The other truly magical thing is that the conversation hasn't ended. I keep thinking that it's done, I talked about it, did my interviews, and that's that. But, the truth is, as I edit this book, more instances keep coming up that inspire me to continue adding what I discover out of this to not only this chapter, but also the entirety of the book. The transformation continues when Mom brings up bipolar disorder and how hard it has been for her in the subtlety of a family walk around the block, without even needing to say "bipolar disorder." It happens when my sister calls me directly and says, "I think Dad's manic and I never know what to do about it," me relating to that, then discussing what we could do to help either Mom or Dad. Also, in the aftermath of the current episode, Mom finally says to Dad *in front of me*, "You were pretty manic at that time; I couldn't have done anything to stop you." None of that has happened as directly before. At least that I was exposed to. I expect the conversations to continue with the trajectory that is my current reality.

I treasure the simple (and most recent) moments above from the conversations I've had so far. They continue compounding.

Some more extraordinary discoveries available out of opening this conversation were/are:

1. Discussing the diagnosis with my family.

2. Hearing the way my brother, sister, and I interpreted and expressed what happened when I was seventeen.

3. Talking about mental illness with others inside of my family.

4. Being able to clarify what bipolar disorder entails for one of my uncles.

5. Gaining perspective on what my interpretations were.

6. Giving myself and others time to explore the bipolar disorder conversation outside of my family.

7. Wondering together with my family on how we can improve as people.

8. Learning my family history.

9. Hearing who my family members are for each other.

10. Listening.

11. Not giving up talking about this, in spite of being afraid.

12. Developing resiliency and a deeper love for my mom and my family.

My family and I have had genuine conversations about things I'd never allowed myself to ask questions about and explore. Dad was able to explore more with me like when he called me and discussed his analysis of an episode as it was happening:

"Jen, did the manic episode cause me to fall down the stairs, or did falling down the stairs cause one of the worst episodes I've had in a long time?"

I had no answer. Who could know? He later told me he found he was manic when he fell down the stairs. He wanted it to be clear that there is a huge difference between falling down *because* you are manic and falling down *when* you are manic. And yet, I distinctly remember that he was coming out of the doctor's office when he called me. I'd never had my dad tell me he was coming out of the doctor's office nor ask me anything close to that *ever*.

I can't even express all of the potential breakthroughs that you could have. I don't know what you and your family haven't talked about, what you have experienced, or what you're scared about. Where I found my peace was when I stepped outside of the fear and said what I needed to say. Maybe my family now sees me as someone who can contribute to this conversation. Maybe I can be trusted because I put myself out there and was able to be vulnerable with my people, and now you, my readers. Maybe I now can handle it because I've been willing to explore it. Maybe I could have handled it the whole time. My awareness of all of this, who I am for my people and who they are for me that I discovered *through these conversations*, is something that I wouldn't change for the world.

What could happen for you?

To be honest, I don't know. It's your life, and I can only say what could happen. You could gain freedom, overcome fear, and have conversations with your family members that you've never had before. You could learn to be okay with what happened with your family members and move forward. You could potentially become aware of yourself, discover something new about yourself or your family, and express yourself if you've held yourself back. You could find a community of people to talk to by beginning to talk about mental illness with others, potentially finding people who have gone through the same thing as you. All of this is possible. And it all depends on *you*.

It's okay to hide from this, and it's okay to be however you want while you deal with this. It's also okay to talk about it. It's okay to have a conversation, even if you're terrified.

Take a look at your own life. What do you actually want? What would you get out of specifically in communicating with your people? I can't answer these questions for you. You have to know what you want with this exploration. And also know that there will be surprises that you don't expect, both positive and negative. Either way, it is a chance to grow, learn, and expand yourself. Take it as it comes.

Reflect for a few minutes on what you desire for you, your family members, and friends.

_____

_____

_____

_____

_____

What do you want your life to look like with your family member diagnosed with bipolar disorder? Be as specific as possible.

_____

_____

_____

_____

_____

_____

What do you wish could happen by talking about bipolar disorder in your family/ with your friends? Think big here. What really would you like to see?

_____

_____

_____

_____

_____

_____

After reflecting, re-read what you wrote above and find the big idea there. Try to write it as a phrase or simply one word.

Mine changes, but currently, it's "letting go."

What's yours?

CHAPTER TEN

Grieve First

THE REST OF THIS SECTION IS ABOUT RELATING to the people in your life through communication. It's about the human connection that we've all been losing. With the incredible infrastructure known as technology, face-to-face conversations can be easily avoided. If you're anything like me, these conversations about bipolar disorder seem urgent. It's nearly impossible to be patient, and that doesn't help. Let yourself breathe.

Although it took a while to see for myself, I realized that there was a sense of loss. I lost something because of the expectations I had when I was a child. I expected:

- My family to talk openly about things

- Support in expressing myself fully

- Not to feel bad about myself for expressing my emotions

- Clarity and explanation

- My dad to trust me to share with me his life experiences

Looking at it now, I see I expected perfection. Whether real, logical, or completely fabricated, I still needed to grieve these losses.

Grief is important. Taking care of yourself is important. I couldn't get over anything if I held on to these expectations and didn't allow myself to grieve the losses of what I wanted for my childhood and my family. Sometimes, grief looks nothing like what we want it to look like.

There are some trends about grief though. According to Grief.com, the stages of grief are:

- Denial
- Anger
- Depression
- Bargaining
- Acceptance

One therapist I went to reminded me that grief is cyclical. It doesn't always go in order. It doesn't always work the way we want it to. It can't work the way we want it to. But, I know you didn't want your life to look like this.

So start there.

Know that your family member didn't want this for their life. I'm sure they didn't want anything to do with mental illness. They didn't want this for their family either. Perhaps they are in the perplexity of where my dad was when he felt socially isolated and disconnected, wondering if he could contribute to his family in spite of this illness. We don't know where they are or what they are thinking about. Or why they did what they did.

And we have to start with you.

Consider the following questions:

What were your expectations for your family in this area?

_____

_____

_____

_____

What do you need to grieve?

_____

_____

_____

_____

What do you think you need to let go of in order to have the conversations you want to?

_____

_____

_____

_____

What stage of grief feels the most present for you right now?

_____

_____

_____

What support do you need from your community?

_____

_____

_____

Find out how you feel. Take the time to reflect on a couple of circumstances in your life regarding this person in your family. Let yourself grieve, even if it is the first time. Just start fresh and see how you feel right now about it. Here are some options to support you in this discovery/reflection about grief:

- Write
- Make voice messages for yourself
- Have conversations with people outside of your family
- Talk to a therapist
- Go to a place with lots of memories
- Go for a walk by yourself
- Let out the "feels" in the way you express them most easily
- Scream in a safe place

There is no "right" way to grieve. We all react differently to what comes up in our lives. If you want to connect with people, use the resources at the end of this book to create relationships with people who want to talk about mental illness. You could also make a list of who is in your community that you could share with. If you feel you don't need people to process this, go to your journal, go for that walk. Reflect on what you need and where you are. And, if you don't know for sure, try them all!

For me, writing and talking about it allowed me to let out the emotions that I needed to. It allowed me to let out the grief I had, and the anger, the denial, and the sadness surrounding what was lost. The hope and prayer that God would do something different, asking, begging for Him to heal my dad (aka bargaining) and then finally, the acceptance that this is what my life is.

It's through writing this book that I reached acceptance. It took this to realize that bipolar disorder will never go away in my family. This isn't a one-and-done experience. And with that, grieving won't be over either. As I learn and discover more of my expectations, I might have to grieve them again. I can also choose to actively lower my expectations for this in my life. That may allow for fear, uncertainty, and confusion to show up in our conversations. It definitely would give me the space to stop judging my family for the way they communicate or interact. Wouldn't it be great to let them simply be?

The grieving process will come up here and definitely in other situations in life, when life doesn't go as planned. Building this practice gives the capacity to allow you to grieve in general, not just with circumstances around bipolar disorder and your family.

Don't be afraid to look at things again either. Sometimes, you will need to take those reflections and make yourself listen/read/talk about them again. I have learned that grief is not linear. You can learn a lot about yourself when you go back and see where you were when you were younger. You can learn a lot when you hear/reflect on the way you talk to your friend about bipolar disorder. So, ask a friend you trust to listen and reflect back to you what emotion you are feeling. Take a second to notice yourself and how you talk about it.

Take Care of You First

You can't always prepare for the conversations that you want to have. You don't really know what will happen for you, whether you'll have the answers you want or not. So, if you feel you can't move forward, just let yourself be stuck and go take care of yourself again. Go for the workout that will get you out of your head, a walk, hang out with a friend, or watch a movie. Get out of yourself for a minute (or longer), before you approach this again.

Be Open and Transparent with Yourself

Which stage of grief are you in currently? It comes and goes and changes all the time. Let yourself be with it. You've been through a lot. You deserve to have that friend support you—you deserve to have someone listen to you—and you deserve to give yourself the time to look at it.

◆ ◆ ◆ ◆ ◆

I'm no expert on grief, but it takes time. So, give yourself time. Give yourself grace in this. And if you need a cheerleader, call me.

CHAPTER ELEVEN

What to Ask

HOW DO YOU EVER DECIDE WHAT YOU SHOULD ASK your family? Great question. If you are looking for advice for before or during a conversation with your family member, that is what this chapter is about.

For me, I analyzed, overanalyzed, and finally decided that I would interview my family members. I also hoped that Dad would tell me I couldn't. You can see my hesitation in showing my "expertise" in this chapter. Did I really know what to ask? No. And, I decided to plan and make the interviews formal and recorded in hopes that my nerves wouldn't get the best of me. So for me, to prepare beforehand made the biggest difference. Because, then, when I worried about how the conversation was going for my family member or me, I had something to fall back on. My lists helped me. I know that may not be as helpful for other people. Your conversations *will* be completely different. *You* know your family. *You* know what may work for you. *You* know that you need to prepare. So listen to yourself. Trust yourself. It seriously doesn't have to look anything like mine. This is your life. How could it?

So, what do you really ask? What I asked was open-ended questions. I wanted to give an opportunity to let people talk about what they feel comfortable talking about. With my uncles, I didn't have as much from my own memory. I didn't know their stories would be focused on before I was born.

One uncle told the story of Dad stacking books when he was a kid or how particular he was painting houses when they worked together. Another told a story of how livid my grandmother was when a counselor implied the family could have done something to set off the manic episode (not much was known at the time about this). The third uncle mentioned how weird he acted right after his diagnosis, not letting things go in a one-on-one basketball game, and even rearranging everything in the medicine cabinet in the middle of the night. And, I learned that my grandpa went to my eldest uncle because he didn't know what to do when Dad had one of his first episodes. That was truly unprecedented! At one point, I had thought my dad had gotten the illness when I was born, and I believed I caused it. From these interviews, I learned *for sure* that wasn't true.

I knew that I didn't want my questions to be too focused until I "figured out" what the person was willing to share. Not that I really knew that either. It took a bit of emotional intelligence and reading each person to take the conversation in the direction that I thought they needed. I could have been extremely wrong.

Bringing it back to you, these people are your family members, so you probably know a little bit about them. It's just important to remember that we don't know everything. Remember the pitfalls from the introduction? Don't fall for "this is it" or "this is over," just because you ask the questions.

So if you decide to write out questions like I did and ask the questions as best as you can, I have a few tips that supported me.

Listen to Yourself

Trust that you know what to do. You already know what to say and who to ask. You have the power within you to understand what you need and how to engage with it. Trust that. You never know what you might learn in these conversations, not just about your family, but about you.

Don't Worry About Being Perfect, Just Do Your Best

Give yourself the space to mess up. We can learn a lot about ourselves and others when we allow ourselves to *not* be perfect. You do it like you do. This is not the time to be hard on yourself. Support yourself and let yourself try.

Be Prepared and Specific

I prepared questions. I asked about specific things. My advice would be to do the same. By preparing, I noticed what I actually wanted to know, and as my family members talked, I gauged what I wanted/needed to say next, which brings up the next piece of advice.

Go with the Flow of the Conversation

Revise as you go. Be flexible. Let their stories paint the next question. By doing this, you let yourself be with them. You let your family member be human. Going with the flow of the conversation brings an opportunity for awkwardness, but also, genuine connection. Don't overstep that.

If you feel defensiveness come up in any of this, don't worry, it's normal. A later chapter will offer suggestions for when that happens. Because to be honest, it will happen. You'll have someone say something about bipolar disorder in a way that isn't as "appropriate" for you, and you react. That's natural, normal, and as much as we would like, isn't preventable. It's bound to happen.

To better prepare for your "interviews," (if you so choose to call them that), I have a couple of guidelines to support.

First, Write Your Goals

What do you want to get out of talking about this with your family members? That essentially is your "why." Why are you doing this?

Setting a goal will help you be clear as you approach this topic with your family. Perhaps it is to have your voice be heard, your opinion validated, or to tell the people who are most important to you what they mean to you. Maybe it is to hear their side, have access to family history, or talk about mental illnesses specifically in your family. Pick one. What's cool about setting a goal is that you can always revise it or add another one.

How do you want the conversation to go? Will it be powerful—will it be expressive—is this a chance for you to be vulnerable? You decide. If you're already nervous about this conversation, you might as well plan for that and reconnect yourself to your reasons for doing it.

Second, Write Your Questions

I will give you a bunch of questions I used with my family members, but sometimes that may just deter you from doing the work yourself. To be honest, my questions could be completely irrelevant to your story. You have to decide what is most important to know *for you*.

What is it that irks you and that you can't get out of your head at night when you want to sleep? What questions have you always wanted to know about bipolar disorder? What do you want to know about the diagnosis, the stigma, the effect on your family member? What fear do you have? Write those down, even if they feel stupid.

If you feel you can't find the answers, try these:

- Journal about it
- Have a conversation with someone you trust
- Ask a friend to write down what they hear you say
- Ask someone about what you have complained about your family member
- Ask your friends what they hear that you wonder about

Sometimes we need someone else's input to get the mind rolling. Don't be afraid to ask for help. Sometimes people see our concerns and can express them better than we can. Don't worry about how it sounds, just ask.

For me, I noticed that I started with who I wanted to ask, and then formulated the questions I had. That should naturally come up as you are brainstorming. Or write your questions first, then organize which person the questions are for. Either way is fine.

Finally, here are the questions that I used. I organized them as follows:

- Uncle Questions
- Brother/Sister Questions
- Mom Questions
- Dad Questions

I changed the "uncle" section to "extended family" because it's not limited to just uncles—I just happen to have a Dad whose family had five boys. I hope these below inspire the questions that you decide to ask your people.

Extended Family Questions

1. What do you remember about when my dad was diagnosed with bipolar disorder?

2. What do you remember about how Grandma and Grandpa responded to it?

3. What was it like for your family back then?

4. What is it like now for you?

5. How do you feel when you know Dad isn't doing well?

6. What do you do or how do you respond?

7. How has your relationship developed with Dad? With Mom?

8. Have you ever seen Dad hospitalized?

9. What type of interaction/conversations have you had with Dad about this?

10. What type of interaction/conversation would you like to have in the future?

11. Are there any fears, worries, struggles that you want to express to Dad or to me?

12. Do you remember any other episodes?

13. What do you want for Dad in the future?

14. How do you want to talk about this with me in the future?

15. Anything else you want to say?

Brother/Sister Questions

1. When did you find out that Dad had the diagnosis?

2. What experiences/major episodes stick out to you regarding Dad's bipolar disorder?

3. What was it like for you when...? (Refer to a specific memory.)

4. Were you ever worried you had it?

5. What has it been like for you with Dad's bipolar disorder?

6. What have you researched about the illness?

7. What would you say is the impact of Dad having this illness on your life?

8. Any particular instances that stuck out to you that you want to talk about?

9. Do you think there is anything specifically that helps Dad in a manic/depressive episode?

10. What have you done to contribute to Mom or Dad when he is in an episode?

11. What kind of communication would you like about his illness within our family?

12. Would you be interested in collaborating more to include new strategies when Dad is in an episode? How could we create/facilitate that?

13. Anything else you want to say or share?

Mom Questions

1. Did you know Dad had this illness when you got married? When did you find out?

2. What impact do you think this has had on your marriage?

3. What do you think the impact is on yourself?

4. How do you think this has affected our family?

5. Any specific instances that made a difference for you?

6. What was it like for you when you couldn't talk about it?

7. What was it like for you when you did? Or what is it like now to talk about it?

8. Who do you see yourself as within our family?

9. How do you think your view of yourself has changed over the years—illness or not?

10. Have you personally experienced mental illness? When/where?

11. How did you deal with all of this?

12. Anything else you want to share?

Dad Questions

The Dad list was too long to include here, so I condensed the questions. Some of them I asked, and many others organically came up in conversation.

1. How and when were you diagnosed?
2. What has the process been like for you?
3. How did you decide that you wanted to wait to talk about it?
4. How has the stigma affected you and your life?
5. How does depression/mania show up for you?
6. How can we support you as a family?
7. What is the best way to be there for you?
8. How can we interact about this in the future?
9. Where do we go from here?
10. Anything else you want to share?

Notice that I always ask the person if they wanted to share anything else at the end of the conversation. I kept those questions in every section because I want you to remember that although you are guiding the conversation, it is about them too. If they have something they want to share with you, let them. It's pretty cool to see what types of things are brought up if we allow someone to share openly and without judgment.

Sometimes I would skip over questions that my family member had already answered in the context of a conversation. And other times, it was awkward, and I didn't know how to ask a particular question or what to say. And, it was all okay. I am lucky to have patient people in my life who were willing to help me when I felt weird. It's all okay especially because it's not perfect.

You decide how it goes for you. Make your own list of what you want to know. The answers to these questions allowed me to understand some trends within my dad's illness and begin to see *again* that Dad is Dad, and the illness is the illness. Once we can connect with those trends, maybe we can understand where bipolar disorder is going and prepare ourselves for what comes next: high, low, or in-between. I can't promise anything though. It depends on your goals, your family, and your communication.

And, however it will go is how it goes. That's it. People become uncomfortable talking about this kind of stuff. It has nothing to do with you. What you do here takes courage. You could be exploring a new way of how you communicate with your family. It could be scary and upsetting. You can do it. You already know what to do that's true to you. So go for it already.

CHAPTER TWELVE

How You Know It's Right: Plan to Get Stopped in Your Communication

YOU WILL KNOW IT'S GOING WELL if you feel like you can't say anything, and you are at a standstill. It's all right. Keep going, one step at a time.

The goal of this chapter is to empower you and your communication skills when you feel like you can't say anything. Many of us have been trained to *not* say anything about mental illness. That's why the stigma still exists. It takes courage to open up, especially when you think you can't. It's an opportunity to push through the fear and do it anyway.

When you're stopped, you can't address what you want to. Now that you clearly know your goals, people you want to talk to, and even the questions you want to ask, you could be teetering on whether it's necessary, or if this is the "right" time, especially if your family member just went through an episode. Will something you say trigger them again? Should you wait? Or maybe you tried talking to your family member, and they shut down, stopped talking, or asked you not to bring it up. Either way, you are stopped.

Take a deep breath and use your best judgment here. We tend to not trust what we know we need to do in these moments. Start there, always.

Then try talking with *someone* about what you are going through. It doesn't have to be your family member. I believe that talking will make the biggest difference in processing what bipolar disorder is and means for you and your family members. Then follow the next couple of steps to remove these barriers and create self-awareness.

Say That You're Stopped

Any of these versions are fine:

- I don't know what to do or say.

- I am uncertain of the future of this conversation about bipolar disorder.

- My family member said something that I take as hurtful.

- I don't want to do this anymore.

By saying it clearly, you may provide yourself with an opportunity to do something else in this circumstance or other ones in the future. That could be all it takes. Otherwise, try what's next.

Take a Minute to Be Aware of Yourself

Use the questions below to help you be honest with yourself as you consider what is stopping you.

1. Where exactly are you stuck?

2. How does it feel?

3. Have you been here before?

4. What did you do last time you were stopped like this?

5. Did it help?

6. Who have you relied on to talk about this?

7. What frustrates you about this situation?

8. What worries do you have?

9. How does this trigger you and why?

10. How do you want to be with your family member while you are feeling this way?

11. How do you want to communicate with them?

12. What is the best way to communicate with this family member?

13. What is the best way to take care of yourself at this moment?

These questions may inspire your next action. Upon reflection and giving it time, it can support you with what your life will look like in the future. By becoming aware of yourself and your habits, you could finally have an option to do something different. So, take the time to reflect. And remember that self-care is just as important as your family member, if not more. You cannot take care of others if you don't take care of you first.

If these questions aren't supporting you, try one of these:

- Be in community (even if you don't say anything)
- Sign up for a support group
- See a therapist
- Check with your family member's doctor (if appropriate)
- Utilize a resource that you feel supports you
- Read a book about bipolar disorder
- Join an online advocacy group
- Sign up for a personal development course to increase your self-awareness
- Meditate or pray about it

Remember to give yourself grace and allow yourself the time to grieve. I have found that once I really take a look at myself and say,

"I am stopped," to someone else, I can see an opening. It may take some time, but being stuck is a chance to discover something new.

With my story, I was the one stopping myself. My negative self-talk, doubting, questioning, and unwillingness to let go of the past brought me much suffering. I noticed when I gave myself the time and when I kept going, even when I felt like it wasn't worth it, that was where I stumbled through a couple more conversations or discovered that no one knew what to do. It can be frustrating to have the same thing stop us over and over, and yet, the pattern is there. Perhaps it has always been there. Where are you stopped in your communication?

There is no escape from communication troubles. We won't always know what to do and may need to ask for help. Remember, no one really knows what to do most of the time. No one can tell you what is *right* or what is right *for you*. Only you know that. Take the time to find what makes sense for you.

Give Yourself Space

Let yourself feel, let yourself not know it all. Let yourself explore with someone you trust (or perhaps a complete stranger, depending on who you are!). You may need time to gain a new perspective. I personally believe that talking it out with someone committed to listening to you gives much power, freedom, and acceptance. And, it's a lot quicker than analyzing in my own brain by myself.

As adults, we rarely give ourselves opportunities for trial and error. We think we should understand it fully the first time. By giving yourself space, you allow yourself to make mistakes. Whether that's with someone else, analyzed in your mind, or on paper, you can let it be. Practice running through the next conversation before you do it, knowing that you may still be nervous when you talk to your family member. Do it anyway. Be patient with yourself.

It may be an hour, a day, a week, or longer, just don't let your "space" take you out completely. Remember, everyone is working together to have your family member succeed: yourself, your doctor, your friends, and your family. That community could also allow you to talk about what you need to before approaching your family member. We have this community and are not alone, so please don't forget that.

Being stopped is a human thing to happen. Keep that in mind as you approach this. Give yourself the grace, acceptance, peace, and understanding, even when you don't want to. These will help you grow and support your person even more than you have been able to in the past. You won't be stopped for long if you're willing to look at why. Say that you're stopped and give yourself some time. It will be worth it in the long run.

CHAPTER THIRTEEN

How to Strengthen Your Communication Skills and Combat Defensiveness

COMMUNICATION, ESPECIALLY WITH FAMILY MEMBERS, can be tricky. You can be frustrated or upset with yourself or others. You can be depressed, anxious, or even defensive. All of these reactions are natural and normal.

I personally think the hardest one to overcome is defensiveness, so I want to take this chapter to talk about it. Because let's be real, when we get defensive, sometimes we can bite people's heads off, and I know I'd prefer not to have that side of me come out too often.

We can feel defensive when we feel under attack. Anything could trigger this defense mechanism. It's automatic, and most of us can't stop it. And, I'm telling you that it's possible to see it in yourself, and control it.

So, how do we practice this when we have such an impulse to have someone off our back? Especially when we're already talking about personal, uncomfortable things? How can you stop yourself from getting defensive when you're about to have more intense conversations with your family members about bipolar disorder? What can you do to decrease your reactions and let whatever happens, happen in the conversation? Here are a few tips:

Take a Deep Breath

Oh, my goodness, your family member just said something that you weren't expecting, and it was exactly about one of your insecurities! You are shocked, you have half a second to respond, and you can feel it bubbling up in your throat. Your reaction. You're getting defensive, and you don't want to. You know that if you do, it could shut out the conversation. Breathe.

Instead of letting yourself react, just take the biggest breath you can. Put yourself on mute if you're on the phone. Or let yourself say, "Give me a minute to respond." That gives you time to feel. And it will get better over time. The first thing to do is to take a deep breath. Breathe.

Sometimes, what your family says can help and support you. And other times, it doesn't. What they say could or could not be what you need them to say to feel heard and understood. As adults, we need to be able to recognize those imperfect communications, and say what we need to without taking things personally. What they are saying is simply another opinion. Remember to listen openly, and let their response to what you ask be simply that: one way to respond.

Acknowledge Your Defensiveness

Say, "I hope this doesn't sound defensive..." or "I don't mean to defend myself here, and..." If you feel the frustration, the upset, the annoying reaction that you are so used to doing, practice saying something like the words above. When I said that, it allowed me to say how I felt without being reactionary. Having someone point out your insecurities or say "how you are" can trigger defensive responses. Someone who's known you since birth could probably tell you a little bit about yourself, and it won't necessarily be wrong or right. It's their perspective of you, that's all.

Practicing saying that you're feeling defensive will give you an option to share your opinion without being confrontational. When both parties are defensive, it doesn't really give room for discovery or understanding. But when you call yourself out on it, it gives others an opportunity to listen to you from outside of that defensiveness and lets them keep their guard down because they have an idea of what could be coming. By saying this, it lets them see defensiveness as an exploration versus an attack. It forewarns them. It's not always possible (believe it or not, you're human too), and it's a good thing to practice for when you feel your defenses coming up.

Be Gracious With Your Response

To be gracious with yourself and gracious in your response is extremely important. Remember that what they have said, even if you feel defensive, is okay. Be open with the people you're talking to, create the loving connection that you intend to. Be gracious in the way that they respond and with yourself. Let yourself stop the conversation if you need to and plan to come back to it. Let yourself feel what you need to feel in the moment. Your responses are telling you something. You can be the bigger person, and you can say what you want to. The goal is to grant yourself permission to communicate. You can empower yourself and move forward through community. Don't be afraid to pause and take a break if you need it. Remember the goals you set before? Keep those in mind, and give yourself and your family members grace.

Practice, Practice, Practice

We can practice every day, every single time that our defenses come up. And, we have the availability to choose to mindfully practice. We can become upset, and we can let ourselves react the way that we usually respond. We get defensive: it can show up as reactionary, angry, and frustrated. For me, as you already know, it becomes tears. For you, it may show up as "overwhelmed," "I don't know what to do," or "confused." Remember, when you mess up, it's okay to go back and say that you messed up. Practice and keep practicing with patience, kindness, and love to yourself and others.

Don't Give Up

Remember, defensiveness is natural and normal. For me, having conversations with my family made the biggest difference in letting go of the impact of this illness on me. When I didn't give up and asked directly for what I wanted, it made the conversations easier— things slid off my back easier, and I didn't have to get mad at myself for not saying anything, again. I wanted the conversation to be available within my family, so I kept talking about it. I keep talking about it. I became better at talking about getting defensive, catching myself, and being less reactive. The defensiveness never goes away. It can shift, but it doesn't disappear.

Remember, the more you allow yourself to bring it up, the more chances you have to reach your goals. Adding questions to your statements like "What do you think?" or "Would you like to say anything about that?" supports people in stating their own opinions and expressing themselves. You can say something, and they do too. Win. Win.

Getting defensive is human. And you'll discover that your defensiveness can change to different responses over time. It is a necessary part of being human. Let yourself feel, breathe, give grace, practice, and say some things that maybe you haven't said before. Try it, and find what works for you.

This is important to you, so it's worth it. It was worth it for me.

CHAPTER FOURTEEN

Discovering Who You Are

ONE IMPORTANT COMPONENT of talking with my family was discovering who I am for them. By knowing and embracing *me*, I gave who I thought I was. At seventeen (and before), I was quiet, shy, reserved, an avid book reader who loved her family and didn't rock the boat. I have changed into someone else as an adult. Friendly and consistent, I worked my way up to being organized, on time, and reliable. And I've always loved my family. That will never change. By knowing who you are as someone malleable, worthy, important, and trustworthy (+ *insert your own positive trait here*), you can interact with the world differently, including within your own family. So here are some tips as to how to understand who you are.

Take Your Time

Patience truly is a virtue that many of us don't have, especially due to the instant gratification we have with the technology of our time (Amazon, smartphones, getting information instantly, and even fast food). By taking the time to develop an awareness of yourself, seeing who you are (and who you can be for that matter) will help you blossom into something beneficial for you and your community. I'm not saying you always do the right things or conversely, that you need to fix something. It's just that we enjoy sticking to our routines and maintaining our habits. That includes sticking to routines that don't support us like constantly being mad with one another, complaining all the time, or not making time for that workout. When you give yourself the time to discover what you want with your family members as you open up this new dialogue, this will empower you even further. Having thought through what you need to beforehand by writing, having conversations with friends (or whatever way makes sense for you), you can know where you stand and what you want to say and do.

Don't Wait Too Long

I wanted to interview my grandparents about their lives when I was in high school. And then, Grandma passed away, and Grandpa had a stroke and never regained full functioning nor talked the way he did before that trip to Africa. I missed my window.

Life is short, and you should do the things you want to do as soon as you can. For me, that meant putting events on the calendar and having accountability partners at my fingertips, setting myself up for success so that when I became upset at something one of my family members said in an interview, I had someone to turn to. As the extravert I am, I sometimes talked with the person in my closest vicinity, usually my coworker. My job as a flight attendant allows for what we call "jump seat confessions," where we share our lives and our experiences or what we are going through while on the jump seat. The heart-crushing and soul searching moments were processed with these coworkers or other close friends.

I let myself feel and be there with my family as it happened in its own time. Through that, I learned what I needed to say next, and I practiced it, over and over. Don't miss the opportunity to make a positive impact in your conversation with your family. It will make a difference not just for you, but also for the friends, family, and coworkers around you. Don't wait.

Really Truly Listen

You can decide how you respond to conversations with your family members. My recommendation is to practice listening and asking clarifying questions. You can practice that at work, home, volunteering, at the grocery store, on a trip, or vacation. Practice everywhere because then you can be there for your family *and* for yourself. By deciding to listen and let go of whatever they say that may offend you or bring up negative thoughts, you can make a positive change for yourself.

In my family, I decided to approach it with love. I saw how they loved me and cared about me, how they'd do anything for me, and it brought me to the confirmation that I wanted to see. I came to the conclusion that I am worth it, and these conversations are worth it, not just because of what they said, but also by letting myself be myself. Listening to others' perspectives as well as myself allowed me to understand, grow, and thoroughly enjoy the life I have now. Not perfectly, but with a mindset that maybe those opinions can help me understand who these people really are in my life.

I hope for the same with where you are.

The Power of Choosing

Choose how you show up when you talk to people in your family. Be brave. Be bold. Be gracious. Be loving. Be peaceful. Pick something you haven't tried before and choose to embody that for the whole conversation. You choose who you are, what you want, and how you talk about mental illness with your family. You can choose how you show love, how you listen, how you react. By embodying this power that you have to choose, you can be however you want to be. By being able to choose, you can have the freedom to live the happy times and learn to let go of the sad, angry, or frustrating ones. The conversations won't be perfect. You're bound to offend someone, not listen, shut down, or feel invalidated about what you say or they say. You can choose how it looks from now on. And never forget that you can call in reinforcements of your community to listen and support you.

Take the Risk

Take the chance on yourself, your family, and your community to talk about this important topic of bipolar disorder. You can be nervous and step into it. You can fail and pick yourself up and keep trying. It was not easy to bring up something when I was told, "You hold onto too much, Jenny," or "You're asking too much," or "Let it go." There's a chance that confronting this will lead to anger, frustration, and exhaustion. Take the risk anyway. And as hard as these conversations can be, I promise you, it will be worth it.

For me, I now see how my family was there for each other, how they interacted, and how our lives intertwined. I can listen for their perspective and validate it as one. That risk was terrifying, but by knowing myself as someone who changes and grows, I grew even more through the experience. I discovered my story and expressed it *fully* for the first time. I used the opportunity to practice what I said and say it again and again, talking to family members about depression, love, bipolar disorder, and betrayal, while simply sharing that particular version of my story with them. I heard for myself uncles' perspectives and the support they were/ are for my dad. I saw the confusion, the clarity, the upset, and the calm.

But I couldn't have if I didn't risk it. The risk is worth it. Go try and epically fail! Or better yet, go try and succeed in having the conversation with your mom about why your parents divorced due to the illness. Talk to your family member without beating around the bush for the first time. Or maybe you guys already talk about it, and you want to simply go deeper. Ask a question you've always wanted to! Try something new! Get out of your comfort zone and risk it all to relate to them in a way you've always dreamed of. It's worth it. Guaranteed.

SECTION III: RESOURCES

Why Include Resources?

IT'S IMPORTANT TO SHARE WHAT WE KNOW. I compiled and analyzed these resources so it would be easier for you and family members. I was where you are. These resources can support you with your experience. They helped me by giving me a couple of things:

- Tangible information and statistics

- Being able to connect emotionally with people who have been there before

- Expressing myself fully

I hope they will do the same for you.

CHAPTER FIFTEEN

How To Research

SO, YOU WANT TO KNOW MORE about the illness, about the treatments, about the families that go through this, and whatever else is on your mind. Research can take you down the endless pit of the internet and not actually help you achieve your goals. Perhaps you've already gotten frustrated.

This is a quick how-to of starting your search.

Write Out Your Goals

I know, again? This is a bit different because this isn't your goals for having conversations about bipolar disorder, but rather goals for *researching* bipolar disorder. Goals are an important step in identifying what the purpose is for you. It is helpful because then you know if you have achieved it, because it is clear and measurable. Some example goals include:

- I want to find three potential doctors for my significant other.

- I want therapy for myself that is reduced priced or free.

- I want to find a support group for myself.

- I want five books that are about a child diagnosed with bipolar disorder.

- I want the statistics for how many people are diagnosed in a year, where they are located, and what their symptoms are.

Just like in conversations, you may get stopped in researching. If you have these written down in a simple place to find, you'll have them to go back to. The more specific your goals, the better. I kept my examples pretty vague, but you can always include a city or state or even a local hospital. Let yourself dream about what you want to find out. It helps.

Make Categories or Lists

Organization isn't everyone's strong suit. I know it wasn't mine. I fall into the depths of the internet for hours watching videos, checking emails, forgetting what I was going to look up in the first place, as I know we all can do. A list organizes your thoughts and keeps the structure in front of you. That helps you find what you need and the guidelines to find what you want out of researching with the time you have.

Stay Focused

It's so easy to become distracted, so set aside the time just for this. If it's five, ten, fifteen minutes, or even an hour, or you use the time while your kid is browsing through library books and you pick up one for yourself, then do it. I'd rather you spend a little bit of time and stay focused than get frustrated and not find anything about what you wanted. Don't try to self-diagnose. Don't try to solve all the problems in your world. Don't try to do it all at the same time. Bite-size pieces can help you chew. Then you digest it, and you'll remember it more. Take it slowly.

Talk About What You Need

This request is bold for those that don't. It can be scary and confronting.

Maybe you do talk about what you are looking for regarding your family member's bipolar disorder. Great! Keep going. If that's you, this part isn't for you.

I'm talking to those who keep it all in, those who don't want to say anything and have trouble asking for it. Start talking and remember that other people are resources too. You can learn a lot from someone else, even if it's not about bipolar disorder specifically. People generally want to share their experiences when they feel comfortable. When you open up, someone else might be able to as well. They may have the perfect solution, but if we don't say anything, we'll never know.

Take a couple of steps in this direction and give yourself grace if you have to take a couple of steps back. Be patient with yourself and others.

By knowing and developing your research skills, you'll be able to learn, grow, and communicate differently about bipolar disorder. Be specific and don't give up. The resources are right in front of you.

Q & A About Bipolar Disorder and Quick Statistics

HERE ARE COMMON QUESTIONS about bipolar disorder and a page with some statistics of the illness. You can then explore other things that could be important to your well-being or your family members.

I have included the references after each question to remind you that they are available for you. Please do your own research too. This is a start to where you can go next as you explore options for you, your family member, and your community.

Q & A About Bipolar Disorder

How exactly is bipolar disorder diagnosed?

For standard mental illness diagnosis and treatment, doctors use the Fifth Edition of the Diagnostic and Statistical Manual of Mental Illness or DSM-5, which is the updated version from 2013. DSM-5 symptoms say that you need certain components to be diagnosed with different types of bipolar disorder, which a specialist can show you in more detail.

How do I know if my family member has bipolar disorder?

The symptoms in DSM-5 will determine whether your family member has bipolar disorder. It is not simple to diagnose. Never try to diagnose someone or yourself. Make sure you understand the illness and focus on finding a good doctor. Bring those concerns and foster a good relationship with that person to develop the right plan of action. Then you and your family member can know for sure, according to what a qualified doctor is trained to do.

How many types of bipolar disorder are there? And what's the difference between them?

Technically, there are four, according to the National Institute of Mental Health (NIMH) nimh.nih.gov:

Bipolar I Disorder—involves episodes of severe mania (increased energy, racing thoughts, and more) that last up to seven days, can have episodes of depression or "mixed episodes" (of both depression and mania symptoms at the same time) but don't have to in order to be diagnosed with bipolar I.

Bipolar II Disorder—depressive episodes as well as hypomania (mild form of mania, hyperactivity, elation)

Cyclothymic Disorder—less extreme shifts in mood, usually does not interfere with daily functions

Other Specified and Unspecified Bipolar and Related Disorders—any bipolar symptoms that don't match the three categories above.

What are the symptoms of mania and depression?

See the DSM-5 criteria for mania, hypomania, and depression for more details.

In general, mania or hypomania has three to four of the following symptoms, according to the DSM-5:

- Increased self-esteem

- Inflated grandiosity

- Less need to sleep

- Talks more than usual

- Thoughts are racing

- Distracted

- Extreme involvement in activities with potential for bad consequences

Depressive episodes show tendencies of:

- Lack of motivation

- Depressed mood

- Weight loss/gain

- Sleep disturbance

- Loss of interest in activities

- Sense of worthlessness

- Inability to concentrate

- Recurrent thoughts of dying

What are treatments for bipolar disorder?

According to WebMd.com, prescription medication treatments can include:

- Mood stabilizers

- Antipsychotics

- Antidepressants

Psychotherapy can be paired with the medications as well.

Psychoeducation also supports learning about the diagnosis so one can be aware of treatment options and others' experiences to find the appropriate support services one needs.

Are there other ways to treat bipolar disorder besides prescription medication?

Psychotherapy such as cognitive-behavioral therapy, interpersonal/social rhythm therapy, group therapy, and family therapy can all support a person diagnosed with bipolar disorder, none of which require prescriptions.

Other alternatives can be found through avid research and taking care of one's well-being. Please see Therapies and Treatments to Research for a more comprehensive list below. And, always consult your doctor to find what is appropriate for your family member in treatment.

Are there certain nationalities that tend to have bipolar disorder?

According to information I found on the International Bipolar Foundation site (ibpf.org), bipolar disorder is not diagnosed as consistently in minority cultures, although it is just as prevalent. Early and accurate diagnoses are the exception, resulting in a discrepancy in treatment and a higher percentage in incarceration, discrimination, and misdiagnosis. (ibpf.org)

What can be done about the stigma related to bipolar disorder?

Talk about it!

Join an advocacy group with the Depression and Bipolar Support Alliance (DBSA), National Alliance on Mental Illness (NAMI), Substance Abuse and Mental Health Services (SAMHSA), or other local bipolar disorder advocacy groups. See the list of websites below that deal with mental illness to see if they have advocacy programs as well.

What laws have been passed related to mental illness?

There are many, and some of the major ones include:

Americans with Disabilities Act (ADA) of 1990, which prohibits discrimination for someone with a disability in jobs, public transportation, and public services. It allows for someone who is discriminated against to take legal action if necessary.

The Rehabilitation Act of 1973, which gave federal provisions for someone diagnosed with a severe disability, giving federal funding to train, research and support vocational rehabilitation services for those with disabilities.

The Mental Health Parity and Addiction Equity Act (MHPAEA) of 2008 requires healthcare providers to treat mental health and substance abuse services as they do with medical/surgical benefits.

The Patient Protection and Affordable Care Act and Health Care and Education Reconciliation Act (collectively known as the Affordable Care Act) of 2010 amended the MHPAEA and made it so that insurers could not discriminate against those with pre-existing conditions by denying coverage or charging higher premiums.

(mhanational.org and cms.gov)

What kind of financial support can I find for my family member diagnosed with a mental illness?

I recommend looking at the government level and at the level of nonprofit organizations.

Some government programs are:

- Medicaid

- Medicare

- Department of Veteran Affairs (VA)1

- Children's Health Insurance Program (CHIP)

- Employee Support Services

- The Substance Abuse and Mental Health Service Administration (SAMHSA)

- MentalHealth.Gov

As far as nonprofit organizations go, see the list of website later in this chapter.

What funding is available for organizations?

Mental Health Block Grants (MHBG) supports building mental health services in communities.

Search the following websites to find more specific funding:

- mhanational.org

- HHS.gov

- thenationalcouncil.org

- nimh.nih.gov

- samhsa.org

- who.int

- nami.org

---

[1] There are many other services that can be provided to veterans. If you qualify for a mental health service and are a veteran, grants are available if you search for them.

What support can I find from my family member's employer?

Always check with your health insurance to see what is offered regarding short/long-term disability programs. Sometimes the human resources department at work can provide extra resources such as support groups, or therapy programs as well.

Remember to use the law to your advantage. If you feel that your family member is being discriminated against, you must advocate using the laws. Please make sure you have researched as best you can and use your community as a resource in searching for support from employers.

What advocacy is already out there related to bipolar disorder?

Many blogs, resources, and advocacy groups are already around! As soon as I started asking for resources, I found them. I found the National Alliance on Mental Illness Family to Family course, which provided me a community-led class based on years of research. Many of the best resources I found were from word-of-mouth, so people around you may have the answer you are looking for.

There are many people and organizations who have been reducing the stigma in their own way. Don't hesitate to get involved in one of the many communities out there already. These tend to be available in many big cities, use a search engine to find one nearest you.

- Other ideas to find mental illness resources/advocacy opportunities:
- Ask questions of your employer/HR department/union representatives
- Search your neighborhoods, in coffee shops, open settings and libraries

- Start a conversation with your neighbor/family member/friends asking for their experiential knowledge

- Do a simple Google search for online groups/forums

How can I get involved with advocacy for mental illnesses?

Reach out! There are so many organizations working on policies, advocacy, support groups and more. Please take one of your strengths and get involved! See the list of websites I have included below, find one that interests you. Some advocacy opportunities include:

- Policy creation and creating laws

- Hands-on support services for those with mental illnesses

- Teaching what you know

- Leading support groups

- Creating fundraisers for nonprofit organizations or other existing programs/advocacy walks

- Volunteering with an existing organization using your professional skill set (website creation, meet & greets, organizational structure, writing, idea creation, etc.)

Quick Statistics

According to the National Institute of Mental Health (NIMH) nimh.nih.gov:

- Bipolar Disorder affects 5.7 million Americans, 2.6% of the population over eighteen years and older.

- The median age of onset is twenty-five years old.

- Two-thirds of people diagnosed have a close family member who also has a diagnosis of bipolar disorder or unipolar depression.

- When manic as children or adolescents, they experience mania as destructive and irritable instead of euphoric and elated in adults. Kids also tend to have physical symptoms of depression (headaches, stomachaches, tiredness) versus what the average adult feels.

- DBSA bipolar disorder statistics from 2000 shows that people with the disorder suffer through as long as ten years of coping with symptoms before being diagnosed accurately. Only one person in four receives an accurate diagnosis in less than three years.

- Bipolar disorder results in 9.2 years reduction in expected life span. Up to one in five people diagnosed with bipolar disorder completes suicide.

- Approximately 83% of cases of bipolar disorder are classified as "severe" nimh.nih.gov/health/statistics/bipolar-disorder.shtml

Emergency and Information Helplines

1. Dial 911—Call if there is an emergency, like harm to self, suicide attempt, or danger to oneself or others.

2. Suicide Prevention Lifeline/Hotline and Veteran's Crisis Line—1-800-273-TALK (8255) for 24/7 support for immediate, confidential, and free counseling.

3. SAMHSA's National Helpline and Treatment Referral Routing Service—1-800-662-HELP (4357) for 24/7 free, confidential treatment and referral information.

4. NAMI Helpline—1-800-950-NAMI (6264) or info@nami.org for a peer support service provided nationwide for people living with a mental illness, their families, and the public, 10 a.m. to 6 p.m. EST.

5. SAMHSA's Disaster Distress Helpline—1-800-985-5990 or text TalkWithUs to 66746 for free, confidential support for those in emotional distress affected by natural or human-caused disasters (tornadoes, hurricanes, drought, wildfire, mass shootings).

6. Mental Health America Hotline/Crisis Text Line—Text MHA or CONNECT to 741741 for 24/7 support for anyone needing mental health services.

7. National Institute of Mental Health (NIMH)—1-866-615-6464 or nimh.nih.gov for phone or live online chat, 8:30 a.m. to 5 p.m. EST.

Books

Bipolar Disorder Memoirs and Personal Narratives

Mimi Baird and Eve Claxton. *He Wanted The Moon: The Madness and Medical Genius of Dr. Perry Baird, and His Daughter's Quest to Know Him.* Broadway Books, 2015.

Terri Cheney. *The Dark Side of Innocence: Growing Up Bipolar.* Atria Books, 2011.

Jessie Close and Pete Earley. *Resilience: Two Sisters and A Story of Mental Illness.* Grand Central Publishing, 2015.

Pete Earley. *Crazy: A Father's Search Through America's Mental Health Madness.* Putnam Adult, 2006.

Adam Grossi. *Wind Through Quiet Tensions.* Candor Arts, 2014.

Stephen P. Hinshaw. *The Years of Silence Are Past: My Father's Life with Bipolar Disorder.* Cambridge University Press, 2002.

Marya Hornbacher. *Madness: A Bipolar Life.* Mariner Books, 2009.

Bassey Ikpi. *I'm Telling the Truth, but I'm Lying.* Harper Perennial, 2019.

Kay Redfield Jamison. *An Unquiet Mind.* 1997.

Paul E. Jones. *The Up and Down Life: The Truth About Bipolar Disorder—the Good, the Bad, and the Funny.* Lynn Sonberg Books, 2008.

Terese Marie Mailhot. *Heart Berries: A Memoir*. Counterpoint, 2018.

Sarah Manguso. *The Guardians: An Elegy*. Straus and Giroux, 2012.

Melody Moezzi. *Haldol and Hyacinths: A Bipolar Life*. Avery/Penguin, 2014.

Sylvia Plath. *The Bell Jar*. Faber and Faber, 1963.

Paul Raeburn. *Acquainted with the Night: A Parent's Quest to Understand Depression and Bipolar Disorder in His Children*. Broadway Books, 2004.

Research and Diagnostic Information

American Psychiatric Association. *Diagnostic and Statistical Manual of Mental Disorders, 5th Edition: DSM-5*. American Psychiatric Publishing, 2013.

Suman Fernando. *Mental Health: Culture, Race, and Ethnicity*. Red Globe Press, 2010.

Frederick K. Goodwin & Kay Redfield Jamison. *Manic Depressive Illness: Bipolar Disorders and Recurrent Depression*. Oxford University Press, 2007.

Hal Marcovitz. *Bipolar Disorders: Diseases and Disorders*. Referencepoint Pr Inc., 2008.

For Families

Xavier Amador. *I Am Not Sick. I Don't Need Help! How to Help Someone With Mental Illness Accept Treatment*. Vida Press, 2011.

Web Burgess. *The Bipolar Handbook: Real-Life Questions with Up-to-Date Answers*. Avery/Penguin, 2006.

Rosalynn R. Carter with Susan K. Golant. *Helping Someone with Mental*. Three Rivers Press, 1999.

Michael T. Compton and Beth Broussard. *The First Episode of Psychosis: A Guide for Patience and Their Families.* Oxford University Press, 2009.

Julie A. Fast and John Preston *Take Charge of Bipolar Disorder: A 4-Step Plan for You and Your Loved Ones to Manage the Illness and Create Lasting Stability.* Warner Wellness, 2006.

Stephen Jacobs. *Mental Illness: A Support Guide for Families and Friends.* 2014.

Harriet P. Lefley. *Family Psychoeducation for Serious Mental Illness.* Oxford University Press, 2009.

Patrick Malone. *The Life You Save: Nine Steps to Finding the Best Medical Care and Avoiding the Worst.* Da Capo Lifelong Books, 2009.

David J. Miklowitz, PhD. *The Bipolar Disorder Survival Guide, Third Edition: What You and Your Family Need to Know.* The Guilford Press, 2019.

Francis Mark Mondimore. *Bipolar Disorder: A Guide for Patients and Families.* Johns Hopkins University Press, 2006.

Jay Neugeboren. *Transforming Madness: New Lives for People Living with Mental Illness.* William Morrow, 1999.

Lloyd I. Sedere, MD. *The Family Guide to Mental Health Care: Advice on Helping Your Loved Ones.* W. W. Norton & Company, 2013.

Ross Szabo. *Behind Happy Faces: Taking Charge of Your Mental Health: A Guide for Young Adults.* Taylor Trade Publishing, 2007.

Linda Tashbook. *Family Guide to Mental Illness and the Law: A Practical Handbook* Oxford University Press, 2018.

For Schizophrenia

Christopher Bollas. *When the Sun Bursts: The Enigma of Schizophrenia.* Yale University Press, 2015.

Donald Capps. *Understanding Psychosis: Issues, Treatments, and Challenges for Sufferers and Their Families.* Rowman & Littlefield Publishers, 2010.

Patrick Cockburn and Henry Cockburn. *Henry's Demons: Living with Schizophrenia, A Father and Son's Story.* Scribner, 2011.

Carol North. *Welcome, Silence: My Triumph over Schizophrenia.* CSS Publishing, 1987.

Elyn R. Saks. *The Center Cannot Hold: My Journey Through Madness.* Hachette Books, 2007.

Pamela Spiro Wagner and Carolyn Spiro. *Divided Minds: Twin Sisters and Their Journey Through Schizophrenia.* St. Martin's Press, 2005.

For Depression and Anxiety

Craig Arthur. *Feeling Alive Again! The Outsider's Guide to Conquering Depression.* 2019.

Kelly Brogan MD and Kristin Loberg. *A Mind of Your Own: The Truth About Depression and How Women Can Heal Their Bodies to Reclaim their Lives.* Harper Thorsons, 2016.

Richard P. Brown and Patricia L. Gerbarg. *The Healing Power of the Breath: Simple Techniques to Reduce Stress and Anxiety, Enhance Concentration, and Balance Your Emotions.* Shambhala, 2012.

Meri Nana-Ama Danquah. *Willow Weep for Me: A Black Woman's Journey Through Depression.* W. W. Norton & Company, 1998.

Matt Haig. *Notes on a Nervous Planet.* Penguin Life, 2018.

Shaun David Hutchinson. *Brave Face: A Memoir*. Simon Pulse, 2019.

Stephen Ilardi. *The Depression Cure: The 6-Step Program to Beat Depression without Drugs*. Da Capo Lifelong Books, 2010.

Harold Koplewicz. *More Than Moody: Recognizing and Treating Adolescent Depression*. Putnam Adult, 2003.

Mathilde Monaque. *Trouble in My Head: A Young Girl's Fight with Depression*. Vermilion, 2007.

Daniel Smith. *Monkey Mind: A Memoir of Anxiety*. Simon & Schuster, 2012.

Gordon H. Smith. *Remembering Garrett: One Family's Battle with a Child's Depression*. Basic Books, 2007.

Andrew Solomon. *The Noonday Demon: An Atlas of Depression*. Scribner, 2015.

William Styron. *Darkness Visible: A Memoir of Madness*. Open Road Media, 1992.

Mark Williams and Danny Penman. *Mindfulness: An Eight-Week Plan for Finding Peace in a Frantic World*. Rodale Books, 2011.

For Borderline Personality Disorder

Susanna Kaysen. *Girl, Interrupted*. Vintage, 1994.

Randi Kreger and James Paul Shirley. *The Stop Walking on Eggshells Workbook: Practical Strategies for Living with Someone Who Has Borderline Personality Disorder*. New Harbinger Publications, 2002.

Jerold J. Kreisman and Hal Straus. *I Hate You—Don't Leave Me: Understanding the Borderline Personality*. TarcherPerigee, 2010.

Rachel Reiland. *Get Me Out of Here: My Recovery from Borderline Personality Disorder* Hazelden Publishing, 2002.

For Out of the Box and Unconventional Thinking

Nadine Artemis. *Renegade Beauty: Reveal and Revive Your Natural Radiance.* North Atlantic Books, 2017.

Stephanie Marohn. *Natural Medicine Guide to Bipolar Disorder: The New Revised Edition.* Hampton Roads Publishing, 2011.

Gary Null, PhD. *The Food-Mood Connection: Nutritional and Environmental Approaches to Mental Health and Physical Wellbeing.* Seven Stories Press, 2008.

Roy Porter. *A Social History of Madness: The World Through the Eyes of the Insane.* Plume, 1989.

Andrew Scull. *Madness in Civilization: A Cultural History of Insanity from the Bible to Freud, from the Madhouse to Modern Medicine.* Princeton University Press, 2016.

Oliver Sacks. *Hallucinations.* Vintage, 2013.

Harriet A. Washington *Infectious Madness: The Surprising Science of How We "Catch" Mental Illness.* Little, Brown Spark, 2015.

Robert Whitaker & Lisa Cosgrove. *Psychiatry Under the Influence: Institutional Corruption, Social Injury, and Prescriptions for Reform.* Palgrave Macmillan, 2015.

Therapeutic Treatments

Monica Ramirez Basco and A. John Rush. *Cognitive-Behavioral Therapy for Bipolar Disorder.* 2007.

Richard P. Brown, Patricia L. Gerbarg, and Philip R. Muskin. *How to Use Herb, Nutrients, and Yoga in Mental Health.* W. W. Norton & Company, 2009.

Mequell W. Buck. *A Guide to Thriving With Mental Illness.* 2015.

Gregory B. Collins and Thomas Culbertson. *Mental Illness and Psychiatric Treatment.* Routledge, 2003.

Leston Havens. *A Safe Place: Laying the Groundwork of Psychotherapy.* Harvard University Press, 1996.

Donald M. Linhorst. *Empowering People with Severe Mental Illness: A Practical Guide.* Oxford University Press, 2005.

Lourie W. Reichenberg and Linda Seligman. *Selecting Effective Treatments: A Comprehensive, Systematic Guide to Treating Mental Disorders.* Wiley, 2016.

Brendon Stubbs and Simon Rosenbaum. *Exercise-Based Interventions for Mental Illness: Physical Activity as Part of Clinical Treatment.* Academic Press, 2018.

Websites

American Psychiatric Association: psychiatry.org or apa.org

American Psychoanalytic Association: apsa.org

APA DSM-5: dsm5.org

APA Practice Guidelines: psych.org/practice/clinical-practice-guidelines

BetterHelp: betterhelp.com

Brain and Behavior Research Foundation (NARSAD): bbrfoundation.org

Bring Change 2 Mind: bringchange2mind.org

Centers For Medicare and Medicaid Services: cms.gov

Centre for Interactive Mental Health Solutions (CIMHS): cimhs.com

Child & Adolescent Bipolar Foundation: cabf.org

Child Mind Institute: childmind.org

Depression and Bipolar Support Alliance (DBSA): dbsalliance.org

Emotions Anonymous: emotionsanonymous.org

International Bipolar Foundation (IBPF): ibpf.org

MentalHelp.Net: An American Addiction Centers Resource: mentalhelp.net

Mental Health America (MHA): mhanational.org

Mental Health Partnerships (MHP): mentalhealthpartnerships.org

MentalHealth.gov: mentalhealth.gov

National Alliance on Mental Illness (NAMI): nami.org

National Council for Behavioral Health: thenationalcouncil.org

National Institute of Mental Health (NIMH): nimh.nih.gov

National Institute on Alcohol Abuse and Alcoholism: niaaa.nih.gov

National Institute on Drug Abuse: drugabuse.gov

National Mental Health Association (NMHA): nmha.org

National Mental Illness Screening Project (NMISP): nmisp.org

National Resource Center on Psychiatric Advance Directives (NRC-PAD): nrc-pad.org

National Suicide Prevention Resource Center: sprc.org/

NeedyMeds.org: needymeds.org

Open Path Psychotherapy Collective: openpathcollective.org

Psych Central: psychcentral.com

Psychiatry Advisor: psychiatryadvisor.com

Psychiatry Online: psychiatryonline.org

Psychology Today: psychologytoday.org

Substance Abuse and Mental Health Services Administration (SAMHSA): samhsa.gov

Suicide Prevention Advocacy Network: spanusa.org

Suicide Prevention Lifeline: suicidepreventionlifeline.org

Suicide Prevention Resource Center: sprc.org

The Depression and Bipolar Support Alliance (DBSA): dbsalliance.org

The Mighty: themighty.com

Trilogy Integrative Services: trilogyir.com

U.S. Department of Health and Human Services: hhs.gov

Wellness Recovery Action Plan (WRAP): mentalhealthrecovery.com

World Health Organization (WHO): who.int

Therapies and Treatments to Research

Case Management or Assertive Community Treatment (ACT)

Cognitive-Behavioral Therapy (CBT)

Dialectical Behavior Therapy (DBT)

Earthing

Electroconvulsive Therapy (ECT)

Eye Movement Desensitization and Reprocessing (EMDR)

Family-Focused Therapy (FFT)

Interpersonal and Social Rhythm Therapy (IPSRT)

Interpersonal Therapy (IPT)

Journaling

Light Therapy

Maintenance Treatment (Continuation Treatment)

Meditation

Mindfulness

Narrative Therapy

Psychoeducation

Psychotherapy

Solution Focused Therapy

Sun Exposure

Transcranial Magnetic Stimulation (TMS)

Vagus or Vagal Nerve Stimulation (VNS)

Accountability Groups, Workshops, and Events For Families and Advocates

Family To Family Course from the National Alliance on Mental Illness (NAMI)—A free twelve-week course made for family members of someone diagnosed with a mental illness.

NAMIWALKS from the National Alliance on Mental Illness—5k walks around the country that raise awareness for mental illness and funds for NAMI work

Behind the Mask Gala from the International Bipolar Foundation—A benefit, auction, and awards dinner to support the organization's programs designed to educate, erase stigma, provide support and fund research for those living with bipolar disorder.

Living Successfully with a Mood Disorder from the Depression and Bipolar Support Alliance—A digital, three-session video course that helps people living with a mood disorder and family members/friends with strategies to succeed with depression/bipolar disorder in treatments, lifestyle and more.

Annual Conference of Mental Health America—Advocacy, policy, discovery of mental health in America for three-day conference.

International Mental Health Research Symposium from the Brain and Behavior Research Foundation—One-day event where experts discuss mental illness research and strategy.

Conclusion

By Jen Kraakevik

HOW DO YOU CONCLUDE SOMETHING that has completely changed your life? This book has morphed my life in this: I can express. I can tell why I was so depressed and talk about if I feel depressed again. Even when fear appears, I don't have to listen to it anymore. Through this book, I practiced talking about bipolar disorder with my family. And, I continue to choose to practice every day I bring up this book in a conversation. It's not over. It won't be over. And as fear wells up again, I know that I can keep talking. When tears stream down, I don't have to make myself stop. I found out through this book that my emotions allow me to connect deeply with others. They are to be cherished and honored, not sloughed away and hidden. Perhaps I have this ability to connect because of how I grew up. Perhaps this was in me all along. So, no more shame or guilt. I can let me be me.

From now on, I can decide how and when and where I interact with bipolar disorder in my family, knowing that it doesn't have to affect my life negatively anymore. It only has made me exactly who I am. That person has now achieved and successfully written a book. I have started conversations and pushed through avoiding, waiting, and wondering. I have asked what I have always wanted to. And as much as I strive to get those conversations and life "right," I can remember that I'm just a person who tries her best.

Through this, I have rediscovered that no one knows exactly what to do. Ever. Even when it seems like everyone else has it together, it is subject to change. We're all discovering who we are newly each day. Even those diagnosed with bipolar disorder. Even our other family members are affected by this illness.

I can *finally* see the community that I've always had. I am *finally* letting my friends and family be there for me in a way I've never allowed them to before. That is the freedom I kept searching for. I hope you provide that same freedom in your communities.

As you embark on your life with what you have understood or seen for yourself from my book, I hope you get to share who you really are with the people in your life. I hope you can see the community we have in being family members of someone diagnosed with bipolar disorder. I hope you have created your own goals, written your own questions, given yourself grace, and perhaps even started your own conversations with your family. I hope you have gleaned something I couldn't have foreseen from this book. Just like what happened for me.

I never could have imagined that writing this would have led me to where I am today. I attribute my story to my wonderful family and their willingness to share and experience this with me. Even when it was challenging to do so.

I wish you the best as you advocate for and love the people with bipolar disorder in your life. Thank you for reading my book and joining me and my family in our discovery, process and thinking. It's an honor to have you read this and I hope it has supported you where you need it most. I can't wait to hear your stories. Thanks for joining my community.

Epilogue

By John Kraakevik

DEPRESSION IS UNINTENDED NARCISSISM. Jen depicted her reactions to my illness well. Her book is a compendium of resources for her voyage through my illness. The most essential one was her experience, which translated much differently than I anticipated.

Bipolar parents know their condition deeply affects the family. They just don't know how. And it is not obvious to either parent or child. Perhaps that was the strongest revelation to me.

I never knew Jen considered suicide. I didn't know she saw a counselor. I didn't know how deeply she was hurt. I didn't know how it affected her relationships as an adult. I knew she had reactions. I wasn't prepared for their depth. Like my own condition, it should have been obvious. But it wasn't.

In the foreword, I asked what I possibly could add to the conversation of mental illness. It was the wrong question. The real question is, how can I listen to hers? And how can she listen to mine? We don't add to the conversation. We add to ours. We all want some sort of closure. Despite all our efforts, neither of us fully understood. And that was somewhat disappointing for us both.

The dialogue continues, and unfortunately, so does the condition. I had two episodes during the course of our writing. Jen continues to ask questions. But the dialogue is deeper and stronger than it was before.

As a result of reading this book, I hope yours is as well.

Call To Action

As you have seen, my family and I decided to share stories together about bipolar disorder. Just like we did, I want to invite you to be a part of our extended family. Your story is important. It makes a difference. I know that we need each other in order to share what has worked with our family members, where we have struggled, and where to go next. This is an opportunity to share resources, make friends, and understand our families even more than we already do.

Please join my dad and me and our extended family on Facebook at: The Impact of an Emotional High Community.

Thanks for being a part of this with us. We love you already and can't wait to meet you there.

Acknowledgements

Dad—for writing, exploring, and showing me how to be with everything related to bipolar disorder.

Mom—for never giving up on our family. Thanks for going through what you did so I could thrive.

Lauren—thank you for being willing to share your life with me and support me every step of the way, even if it isn't easy. Love you.

Dan—for being the rock I needed when we were growing up and even now. I'm so lucky to have a brother like you.

Tom, Tim, Joel, and Steve—for exposing your thoughts and emotions so that I could share mine with the world. Thank you for trusting me.

Craig Arthur—for endless accountability, recreation, opportunities to let go, and for being an endless best friend, thank you.

Susie Goodwin—for being my go-to and always believing in me so I believe in myself.

Greg—for being a contributing angel and believing in me no matter what.

Katie Romich—for the countless opportunities for conversation, helping me reach my potential as a leader, and pushing me to my limits.

Jon—for falling in love with me during the process, always encouraging me to take time to finish this, and supporting me no matter what. I love you so much.

PJ—"Who knew we were destined for each other?" A million thanks.

Mary Ann—thank you for the encouragement, access to accountability in community, and inspiration from the beginning. Without you, I wouldn't have even started on this path. Thank you.

My flying partners, all who listened and asked questions about the printed manuscripts I brought on planes—thank you for guiding and nurturing me into the person I am now. This book wouldn't be here without your inspiration.

The Wisdom Writers' Guild—Jill, Lori, Evan, Mary Ann, Rebekah, Monica, etc.—for the structure, the check-ins, the coaching, the hours you poured into writing accountability, and your incredibly generous listening.

My Landmark community—for coaching me before I was willing to go here.

Amy Collette and Positively Powered Authors—for grounding and encouraging me in editing and publishing this personal story. I couldn't have done it without the inspiration of you and our community.

About the Author

JEN KRAAKEVIK IS A THOUGHT TRANSFORMER whose goal is to eradicate the stigma surrounding bipolar disorder and open the conversation about mental illness in American society. As someone who can relate to everyone on some level, Jen is skilled in emotional connection, and has a passion for people.

Jen is a writer, a leader, and an advocate for human rights in her workplace union, and provides excellent customer service as a flight attendant. She loves to be outside hiking and biking, and to spend time with friends and family. She currently resides in Chicago, Illinois.

Contact the author at The Impact of an Emotional High Community on Facebook.